Regeneration in Jesus 101

Regeneration in Jesus 101
The ABC's of Spirit Life

D. E. DAVIS

RESOURCE *Publications* • Eugene, Oregon

REGENERATION IN JESUS 101
The ABC's of Spirit Life

Copyright © 2025 D. E. Davis. All rights reserved. Except for brief quotations in critical publications or reviews, no part of this book may be reproduced in any manner without prior written permission from the publisher. Write: Permissions, Wipf and Stock Publishers, 199 W. 8th Ave., Suite 3, Eugene, OR 97401.

Resource Publications
An Imprint of Wipf and Stock Publishers
199 W. 8th Ave., Suite 3
Eugene, OR 97401

www.wipfandstock.com

PAPERBACK ISBN: 979-8-3852-5169-8
HARDCOVER ISBN: 979-8-3852-5170-4
EBOOK ISBN: 979-8-3852-5171-1

03/17/26

Scripture quotations taken from (NASB®) New American Standard Bible®, Copyright ©2020 by The Lockman Foundation. Used by permission. All rights reserved. www.lockman.org

Dedicated to our grandchildren, the eleven songs from the mountain: Landon, Malachi, Selah, Nathan, Finnegan, Iona, Micah, Bella, Eirlys, Moses, and Ava.

Contents

Acknowledgments | ix

Introduction | xi

A is for the Azure Sky | 1

B is for Beatitudes | 5

C is for Contentment | 11

D is for Defying Death | 16

E is for Evergreen | 20

F is for Flying Free | 24

G is for Guidance through the Gauntlet | 29

H is for the Heart | 33

I is for Illumination | 39

J is for Jesus, the Judge | 45

K is for Kingdom Kin | 50

L is for the Life in Jesus's Spirit | 55

M is for the Meaning of Real | 58

N is for Nascent Strength | 62

O is for Open-ended Obedience | 67

P is for Purpose to Profess | 72

Q is for Quantum Entanglement | 77

R is for Righteousness | 83

Contents

S is for the Sacred Union | 89

T is for Transforming Truth | 94

U is for the Ultimate Good Time | 99

V is for Vessels of the Holy Spirit | 104

W is for Wrestling with God | 110

X is for Christ, as in Xmas | 115

Y is for Your Life is Hidden | 120

Z is for Zummary | 129

Bibliography | 137

Acknowledgments

REGENERATION IN JESUS 101 is the result of an idea that occurred to me soon after retiring from a career as an educator, which was to write a book about being a Christian for my grandchildren. The completion of this book was made possible by the help of Linda Baker, a friend from high school from over fifty years ago and a fellow educator, who read the developing manuscript and gave valuable feedback. I also acknowledge Clay McLean, a friend for over thirty years, with whom I have enjoyed many conversations about walking with Jesus. His encouragement to write has been effective. Last, I acknowledge the love and support of my wife, Freida. She has always been and remains the great gift God gave me a year after I received the revelation of Jesus Christ, the begotten Son of God, the Messiah of the Jews, and the Savior of the World.

Introduction

IMAGINE THAT A GIFT of an airplane came to you unexpectedly. The giver says simply, "Because I love you and desire for you to know the joy of flight, please accept the airplane." Astounded and excited, you agree. The plane is delivered to your front yard. What happens next?

Imagine further that all your neighbors are offered the same gift. There are four responses among them. A few reject the gift. They announce distrust of the giver and claim the plane will not fly.

A second response is the neighbors who receive the plane but leave it parked in the front yard as proof they own it. There the plane sits. These neighbors speak of owning it, wash it regularly, walk around it proudly, but never use the plane.

The next response is awkward, yet it is the choice of most of the neighbors; the plane is driven over roads like a car. These plane owners never learn to pilot a plane, and riding in it feels like logical use, though missing the opportunity to fly is illogical.

Observing all the above, the clearly appropriate use of the gift requires learning how to fly. In a matter of time, the lessons pay off. The gift fulfills the giver's intended use and becomes the source of your knowing the joy of flight.

Being a Christian is a bit like receiving the gift of an airplane. Salvation is a two-fold experience. The atonement means our sins are forgiven. Our redemption is the birth in the Spirit—being born again—and the new creature is freed from the sin nature. Walking in the new spirit nature born of God requires understanding and practice. The Father in his wisdom supports our redeemed state by giving the gift of the Holy Spirit to teach and comfort us in the journey beyond our deliverance from the sin nature. The

INTRODUCTION

plane in the analogy above is the new creature spirit. We need lessons in being the new creature. The Holy Spirit teaches us to fly in the spirit.

Luke 11:9–13 records Jesus saying, "Ask, and it will be given to you; seek, and you will find; knock, and it will be opened to you. For everyone who asks, receives; and he who seeks, finds; and to him who knocks, it will be opened. Now suppose one of you fathers is asked by his son for a fish; he will not give him a snake instead of a fish, will he? Or if he is asked for an egg, he will not give him a scorpion, will he? If you then, being evil, know how to give good gifts to your children, how much more will your heavenly Father give the Holy Spirit to those who ask Him?"

Just as one can learn to pilot a plane, *Regeneration in Jesus 101* posits how we may understand the walk of faith as a continual learning of the new spirit being through an active engagement of the Holy Spirit.

An airplane could not be a metaphor used by the prophet Isaiah. He nonetheless is recorded as saying in Isaiah 40:31, "Yet those who wait for the Lord will gain new strength; they will mount up with wings like eagles, they will run and not get tired, they will walk and not become weary."

Now to the ABC's of spirit life.

A is for the Azure Sky
Apocalypse, Altruism, Authenticity

WARNINGS OF THREATS FROM massive solar winds and more war in the Middle East are in the news this week. The climate is changing, and there is debate over whether human activity is the cause. In the news today, an iceberg larger than New York City broke off an Antarctic ice shelf.[1] The United States suffers from a culture war over ideals. Nations have enemies, and allied countries spy on one another. The major economies of the global market generate massive wealth. Civil unrest in the United States springs up, and people lament poverty existing in the midst of tremendous wealth. The scientific community, political think tanks, corporations, and across social media, people speak of the planetary dangers we face. The twenty-first century is a time of turmoil and unprecedented threats.

Humans fear an apocalypse. Apocalypse is a fancy word, isn't it? Like many words, multiple definitions exist. Here are three to consider:

1. "one of the Jewish and Christian writings of 200 BC to AD 150 marked by pseudonymity, symbolic imagery, and the expectation of an imminent cosmic cataclysm in which God destroys the ruling powers of evil and raises the righteous to life in a messianic kingdom"
2. "something viewed as a prophetic revelation"
3. "a great disaster."[2]

Eight billion people on this planet face the mega-threats of pandemics, famines, wars, and economic collapse. Are we facing the end of the world? No. We face the return of Jesus Christ as prophesied in "The Revelation,"

---

1. ESA, "Giant Iceberg."
2. Merriam-Webster, *apocalypse*, 54.

the first definition above (Rev 19:11–16).[3] One Greek word, *apokalupsis*, is translated into the Bible title, "Revelation" and is the root of the English word *apocalypse*.[4]

Two concepts thread through this book. First, all humans share a universal experience of facing the challenges of life in the material world. We ponder what it all means. The second thread relates the Bible to our lives on Earth during this period of history.

On being human, I write to increase understanding of the universal human experience. Examples of the universal knowledge humans share are love, hate, desire, fear, and the challenge of making provision for our bodies. Many find these current days a frightening time; I admit times when fear interrupted my emotional state. I write from a desire for Christian teens to explore the depth of meaning and revelation in the Bible that expands and strengthens any human's experience of faith, hope, and love.

On relating the Bible, I write of analyzing life and one's individual situation by hearing the full biblical message. I believe the deep questions we all face find substantive answers in the Bible; answers unlike any other spiritual teachings. Let's jump straight into *religion*, a consistent piece of the human puzzle since civilizations developed. From the Egyptian god Ra through the religions of the world today, conceptualized and codified propositions of a supreme deity have intertwined with or been the power structure of government. If the reader is a teen from a Christian home, you have heard your parents speak of God and make choices based on believing in Jesus as God.

Think about another "A" word, *altruism*, the "unselfish concern for or devotion to the welfare of others."[5] I bring this up to illustrate a fact many find hard to grasp: to understand our experience as humans and as citizens of the U.S., it helps to separate faith in a living God from religious practices directed toward a deity.

Altruism is both an attitude and an action. It is taught in many religions. An example of altruism being taught across multiple religions is the Golden Rule. Some version of the Golden Rule can be found in Buddhism, Christianity, Confucianism, Islam, Judaism, Taoism, and Zoroastrianism (mentioning the last one just because it's a cool word), to name a few. There

---

3. Paraphrases adapted from the New American Standard Bible: ©2020 by the Lockman Foundation.

4. McEvoy, *apokalupsis*.

5. Merriam-Webster, *altruism*, 34.

are people who believe no deity exists but will affirm belief in the value of altruism.

Practicing altruism may or may not spring from a belief system built around the responsibility to care for others as a function of serving the purposes of a supreme deity. Another reason to be altruistic is to project an appearance of good character. In this crazy world, people gain and maintain political power by vowing that their motivation to hold power is based on a particular set of values or morals. Altruism is a concept often espoused as the reason for a particular political platform, and the intent is to sway public opinion favorably. No doubt, we all scratch our heads when an individual declares a deity figure as the source of their personal values, but their actions include negative verbal attacks on anyone holding opposing points of view on important social issues. In other words, their altruism is a manipulative device not a sincere caring for people in general. Openly prejudicial, inauthentic behavior claimed by people declaring good intentions is rampant.

There are two personal values that combat the negative power of prejudice. First, choose loving others as a deeply held value. Second, learn and practice that choice authentically. Authentic people exude a sense of stability rooted in their character. We might even disagree with the content of someone's words, but nonetheless, recognize the individual's integrity. Integrity is the solid connection between one's stated beliefs and actions.

Now here is a kicker of an idea, and this is the sort of thing that makes understanding life as a human kind of discombobulating. Do not be surprised when someone claims being "true to myself" as justification for their meanness. A person can be authentic to their beliefs, but those beliefs smell rotten. For now, we have simply examined basic authenticity. The next chapter examines individual beliefs.

Authenticity means people are clearly themselves, speak honestly from within, and can be trusted to honor the values they believe in. Being an authentic Christian means you accept loving others as one of your highest aspirations. The authentic Christian experience develops your motives and understanding in line with the biblical revelation of God. Loving others is the core reality of the authentic Christian life, which is the profound experience of the Holy Spirit within one's heart. *Spirit* is not a material world word, yet it is not as hard to grasp as it sometimes seems. The non-material world includes things like one's imagination, hopes, dreams, thoughts, feelings, ideas, and concepts. The words printed solidly on a page are material, but thinking about the words and how they work to build our understanding is not something solid to hold in the hand. *Spirit* as a term, represents many differing usages. There are applications to individuals, groups, and circumstances throughout culture. The biblical usages are the reason for writing *Regeneration in Jesus 101*.

Being a Christian is the practice of knowing the indwelling Spirit or Presence of God. To live by knowing the Presence of the Holy Spirit within you is a discipline. An authentic man or woman who acknowledges Jesus as God develops as someone who loves in all circumstances. We have the Bible, and it reveals the key to life. We have the Holy Spirit, and he guides us into all truth.

Imagine standing outside on a warm and cloudless day. The sky above is a brilliant azure. As you peer into that endless sky, there is nothing but color to be seen, an all-encompassing color intangible yet vibrant. Reality seen by the eye appears as an empty-looking color. Yet, it is the reality of substance true to physics. Light passes through an invisible atmosphere, which has mass and thus can be weighed. The sky is full of the material atmosphere. Light makes the atmosphere appear blue. The expanse of sky is at once boundlessly full but nothing you might grasp in your hand.

The Lord God is real, like the sky. You will see no physical form of him in the material world, but he is real. He is not held in one's hand; he is spirit (John 4:24). You have a body, but you are far more than that body. You are also your thought life; and deeper than those thoughts, you are an inner knowing and feeling. You are an eternal soul. When the light of God fills a person, there is an inner experience with God. The inner being may "see" the Lord; and in that level of seeing—and only there—your inner being knows the fullness of its identity. The reason is clear. In his plan, the part of you that is eternal opens to the truth, and love streams like a river from his heart. He is your Creator and releases within you your authentic self.

B is for Beatitudes
Behavior, Burden, Belief

HUMAN BEHAVIOR IS COMPLICATED. Science analyzes human behavior and creates explanations for people's actions. Human behavior is the subject of an entire scientific branch of study known as psychology, which focuses on the connection between the mind and behavior. Psychological research develops knowledge and insight into aspects of being human, such as personality, attitude, emotion, prejudice, reasoning, frustration, and deviance. This list could easily be expanded.

All day, every day, people around us and we ourselves choose from multiple internal motivations. Behavior is not always a directed choice; many behaviors are spontaneous reactions to the circumstances pressing on us. Humans will react in the moment, as if "bent" in certain ways. Consider personality traits such as creativity or curiosity. In observing others and oneself, it is clear that people tend to just be certain particular traits. These innate attributes often manifest in children before they are old enough to make carefully reasoned choices.

Personality traits can be positive or negative. Arrogance, for example, is considered a negative trait. It is related to something we all feel to some degree: pride. A universal human experience is to feel proud of one's personal accomplishments. We expect a person to smile and experience some degree of satisfaction when an accomplishment brings about positive results. However, arrogance over one's abilities and accomplishments is regarded as a negative personality trait.

Personality traits may appear positive in one person and negative in another. Consider the person who seems determined to achieve. We tend to think of this as a positive trait. However, add selfishness, and that determination may be labeled uncaring or even aggressive. The difference is whether a person expresses strength while maintaining thoughtful regard for others or pushes them aside. Opposite expressions of a common human characteristic like determination are functions of thought-emotion states within a person. Complexities to sort out abound.

The natural world we live in is based on a positive and negative balance: protons and electrons; north and south poles of a magnetic field; for every action, there is an equal and opposite reaction, and so on. In the realm of human thinking and feeling, positive and negative behaviors mirror this opposition-tension. We humans have positive and negative moods, feelings, and resulting actions. Criminal behaviors, heroic behaviors, and the in-between form the landscape of human behavior, from abhorrent to inspirational.

Other people's behavior can be a burden. We sometimes realize we ourselves behave in ways that burden others. The expectations of culture upon us to behave in particular ways are burdensome as well. We can't look inside the motivations of others, at least not clearly, and often we cannot understand our own inner motives.

Universally across the planet, behavior boils down to the definition of what is good and bad behavior. Each culture has expected or acceptable behaviors and rejects behaviors labeled as bad. Basic commonly held beliefs define the goodness and badness of behavior. People become labeled by designations of "good" or "bad" according to their actions. Learning the rules of one's own culture and keeping them is one of the responsibilities of being a member of any given culture. Social expectations may shape us for the better, or we may view those expectations as burdensome and reject them.

What is considered good or bad is a moral judgment. Cultural disagreement in the United States abounds over whether some behaviors are good or bad. These discussions frequently center around relationships, wealth, and social order. U.S. citizens strongly disagree over the topic of morality.

Religions are specific about what behaviors are considered good or bad. Religion usually adds the idea that God will look upon a person's behavior and reward or punish accordingly. Yet, those without religion still have standards of what is right or wrong in their belief systems.

Religion-based or not, rules typically describe rewards that follow good deeds and punishments deserved for bad deeds. This dichotomy is presented in varying degrees to young people through parents and schools.

No doubt, rewards and incentives for right behavior and consequences incurred for not behaving within the expectations have been experienced by us all. Behaving well can be a burden, but behaving badly is even more so—especially when the perpetrator is caught.

Entering the age considered young adulthood means adopting roles and responsibilities within an established culture. From colonial times forward, U.S. culture reflected a common notion of good and bad based on Christian moral tradition. Our institutions and laws have reflected a historical development known as Western Civilization. Within this cultural phenomenon, the reasoning of what is good and bad largely stood on the Bible and church influence.

In my lifetime this has changed. Teenagers today enter a world where many criticize any religious moral ethos and identify all religion as an evil needing to be eradicated. Because humans are inherently flawed, the historically developed Christian religion has often fallen short of the ideals and values taught in the Scriptures. This is another complex topic that Christian teenagers must navigate. Complications can be burdensome.

Much of the discord within the organized church and general culture stems from differing standards of right and wrong. Our Heavenly Father revealed to Adam and Eve that knowledge of good and evil must be avoided. Human beings cannot agree on the standards delineating what is good and what is bad. The new life we enter as regenerated humans is the state that God intended for humanity at Creation. Out of love for him, we receive his Presence, the Tree of Life, and thus the believer is equipped to overcome evil.

A common mantra of this world is simply, "Believe in yourself." This is the moral substitute the world system offers for moral guidance. It is beguiling to think believing in your own abilities and strength is the simple meaning of right and wrong. Warning, it is a false truth that sounds good but will ensnare the soul.

The ideal of believing in oneself promotes living by a limited, even blind, guiding principle. Belief in self limits an individual's spiritual insight within the finite perspective of human capacity. There are many philosophies, self-help notions, and dogmas from the East and West that teach living a meaningful and satisfying life happens by centering on the self. Don't be fooled by labels. Learn to spot this falsehood of being centered on self. It is the source of all selfishness, which is given a palatable lie for a name.

As a regenerated human, we find ourselves open to the pursuit of the highest, most perfect truth, an intellectual knowledge of and emotional reliance upon the living Jesus Christ, Lord of the universe. He is the all in all available to every human being. The Scriptures of both Old and New Testaments are a composite revelation of Jesus.

The New Testament specifically teaches spirit-life as the center of being in the will of the Lord. God intends for humans to be filled with his life by his Spirit, held within the inner being. Spirit-life is not religion, though religions may speak of it. The test of whether a person's words are rooted in the spirit of Jesus is when the fruit of life in the spirit—love, joy, peace, patience, kindness, goodness, faithfulness, gentleness, and self-control—are evidenced by the speaker. Christian religions teach that we should see this fruit in the behavior of Christians. Trying to produce the fruits of the Spirit without drawing life from the root of the vine, the Holy Spirit of the Lord, will be frustrating regardless of the religious dogma. However, that is part of the learning curve, and why the Christian walk is a journey. It takes making errors from self-reliance or from religious tradition to learn how to rely upon him.

Our reactions to people and circumstances are governed by our emotional framework and our belief system. While the emotions are ingrained, our belief system is a function of choice. The arc of one's life develops from decision-making as either the natural self without God or the self born of the divine Spirit, the second birth frequently labeled *born again*. The latter is God's redemptive plan for humanity. We might categorize all basic belief systems as follows:

- Believe in yourself.
- Believe in a moral code such as a religion, a spiritual practice, cultural mores, or government mandate (authoritarian governments indoctrinate their populations that the individual lives for the state).
- Believe in some combination of the first two points above.
- Place faith in Jesus Christ and his revelatory spiritual teaching.

The experience of going to a Christian church may be merely the following of a moral code and not the actual spiritual existence God intends. Mental, emotional, and physical focus on the living Spirit of Jesus lifts a person to the pinnacle of human experience found in the Presence of the Father and Son and stemming from within one's heart by the Holy Spirit.

B is for Beatitudes

No person will achieve spiritual maturity by applying the mandates of any human system on the outer human. In other words, rules may help society function, but keeping rules—even religious ones—is not the holy existence that the Lord God provides for a human being.

The life guided by the Holy Spirit, as revealed in the Bible, is the only holy way God ordains. The Bible calls it the narrow way. All other sources of belief, no matter how these are labeled, are false and will lead you away from the Presence of the Lord and your best life. Right or righteous behavior results when we align our inner motives with the love of God. Everyone is being guided by a spiritually aligned set of perspectives and attitudes. Focus on believing in oneself results in self-built confidence, which frequently spawns self-righteousness. The self lifted up as the goal of being an individual is spiritual blindness. Focus on his Spirit within and experience the truth, peace, and joy in life.

Read the opening to the "Sermon on the Mount" found in Matthew 5. This is a famous set of statements known collectively as the "Beatitudes." I believe in Jesus because no other voice in history has said words as powerful as those spoken by Jesus. The Beatitudes stand as one example of his singular human expression of spiritual truth.

Core truth components of holy behavior are found in the Beatitudes. Being "poor" in spirit is an honest appraisal of one's self-hood as meager and needing God's Spirit. Life is hard, and we often are reduced to mourning over loss—our own and that we see in others. God is faithful to pick us up from the depths of mourning. Gentleness as a choice is often bypassed, but it comes with an incredible promise. Those who hunger and thirst for righteousness find satisfaction. True satisfaction isn't in the behaviors of gaining more stuff, winning glory for skills, or even random acts of kindness. Satisfaction is a deep soul issue, and only life in the Spirit of God will truly satisfy a person across a lifetime. Mercy is a powerful emotional behavior that chooses love as acts of forbearance and forgiveness. Purity in the heart is a state received by inviting the Holy Spirit into one's being. This opens the eyes of the heart to the Lord God, and being enabled to see his hand at work is wondrous (Eph 1:18).[1] From such a solid position of understanding—the "seeing" of God—does the believing one enter the grace to bring peace among others. What a blessed and powerful state needed by all.

---

1. Paraphrases adapted from the New American Standard Bible: ©2020 by the Lockman Foundation.

All the behavior which threads the Beatitudes comes with a cost. The believer who learns to live in the behaviors of the Beatitudes exhibits a goodness which ironically is hated by the darkness in human hearts. All who walk in these ways will be scorned. Yet, emotional beauty and power shine in the Beatitudes. Citizenship in the kingdom of God is not righteousness certified by merely knowing the Scriptures that speak of it. Citizens of heaven are beings of a different culture, distinct from anything that humankind produces. The Earth groans to see true humanity as intended in the creation and the kingdom of God culture evidenced by Holy Spirit-guided relational behavior. This is the wonder of the Gospel at work—God in us, light and love from heaven, lifting us into the profound in-the-spirit experience.

C is for Contentment
Culture, Conundrum, Conscience

CULTURES RESULT FROM HUMAN interactions characterized by a common language, manners, literature, arts, and architecture. Cultures influence each member participant through macro and micro-level functions. A country's flag is an excellent example of these two levels of force. The macro force of a flag results from prolific displays on government buildings, significant social institutions, and private property; these are markers of a cultural status quo. The flag represents the cohesion of experience and values across the culture and as a heritage across time. The micro force of a flag is its power to manifest particular feelings in an individual about the culture. Humans direct the development of children through direct instruction on the macro level, which comprises the seen and known aspects of any given culture, and on the micro level through the inculcation of values that may or may not represent a cultural norm.

An additional source of influence on youth is one's friends. Most families will discuss peer pressure leading to poor choices. Peer pressure is the cultural phenomenon of adopting a friend's opinions favoring a particular value, wardrobe, speech affectation, or set of attitudes. Adults may also be influenced by peer pressure. An example is the desire to have a new car for the sake of appearing more prosperous. Teens, though, are particularly vulnerable to peer influence. Teens are confronting culture and broadening their personal experiences of being human.

The emotional territory of change brought on by developing into an adult spurs a desire for more autonomy in decision-making. Parents and their offspring must navigate the transfer from parental authority to independent decision-making. Peer pressure is just one of the forces that must be understood and navigated on the path to adulthood.

We all experience an inner emotional need for acceptance and affirmation from people with whom we feel an attachment. We need someone, anyone, to value us. I discuss this to help you develop self-awareness of the power of affirmations, which translates within popular culture into the need to be "cool" among a group of peers. (There are assorted contemporary slang words for cool; consider *dope* for an example.) Both healthy and poor choices breed in our hearts according to the group from which we seek affirmation. Becoming an authentic person occurs partly by learning not to act on motivations rooted in the need for affirmations from others. Maturation of our inner sense of being whole and worthy of assurance means learning independent thinking. Independence is one measure of control over one's individual feelings. Conformity provides a sense of belonging, but one must define a group's values carefully before seeking a nod of approval from its members.

A social issue of U.S. culture is our diversity as a nation. In addition to ethnic groups, there is a great divide between political groups, further splintered by diverse social groupings. A challenge for our Christian subculture exists in how we interact with other groups. Often, cultural groups form around sinful behavior. Many sinful behaviors have gained the tacit sanction of the overall culture. Many voices within U.S. culture censure Christian perspectives because we identify some human choices as sin, which the culture labels as personal freedom.

A conundrum emerges. All people in the culture should be respected and accepted by Christians. Yet, some behaviors that humans embrace are against the holiness of the Lord God. The Lord does not approve of all human behaviors. The answer to this conundrum is simple: as Christians, we move away from our culture's pressure to conform to sin but do so without condemning individuals. We think independently of culture and in harmony with God's heart.

When we accept Christ's atonement, which is his repair of our damaging offenses against God, we receive the divine nature of God Almighty as the new substance of our very being. As clear as a warm April morning after a night of spring storms, we are freed from the dark night of our old nature and its selfish behaviors. We enter salvation and discover our power of choice. God renews within us the humanity established at the onset of creation, and we walk on a new path by developing new thought patterns. The key to understanding how this can actually happen is the recognition of the responsibility to choose daily the state of walking in the new nature.

C is for Contentment

We learn to discern between Christlikeness and culture without attacking people for their sinfulness. It is basic logic; we are all sinners. Those who live in the fallen nature must be viewed as our fellow humans but as those who are blinded by darkness. Some who claim Christ fall into a pattern of condemning people who are blinded by deception. The clear teaching of Scripture is not to judge those outside the Christian community (1 Cor 5:12–13).[1] Meanness directed at those with whom we disagree is not a Christian stance.

The conundrum is resolved by the effective communication of God's rejection of evil, spoken clearly as God's solution for overcoming blindness. The stated solution must be backed up by evidence of an authentic difference in the spirit of the believing speaker. We communicate our message of salvation through Jesus by using tonal effects and empathetic understanding, all spoken sincerely from an inner reality of being in the Spirit of Christ.

Denominations with conflicting theological positions often turn the pure river of spirit life into a murky flow. Open your eyes and see the uproar within Christianity for what it is: confusion growing out of the deceitfulness of sin. I urge you to make your faith simple. Start with the words of Jesus and build meaning from all other verses as centered on Jesus. Use a Bible with the words of Jesus printed in red. Fellowship where you sense the leading of the Lord, but remember your allegiance is to Jesus, not a particular interpretation of Scripture. Develop devotion to God. In a pure commitment to Jesus, the spirit of Jesus shines through in truth, with love for both fallen and redeemed—synonymous with renewed—humans. The meaning of truth and love unveils the wondrous beauty of God. When a person follows Jesus as the way, the truth, and the life, everything else about living on earth in these times takes on meaning and substance.

If a qualifying adjective precedes the word "gospel," it may be immediately recognized that a conjecture of opinion stands on a dogmatic teaching. An example, but certainly not the only one, is the Prosperity Gospel. The twist of meaning upon Scripture is clear. Being prosperous defines how the gospel is taught and received. The good news of God with us—of salvation coming to us, of comfort and guidance through the Holy Spirit, of the end of the story being the reign of the kingdom of God on earth—is profound. It needs no slant in any direction. Be patient and not carried away by doctrines or teachings that offer a "better" interpretation (Eph 4:14). Understanding

---

1. Paraphrases adapted from the New American Standard Bible: ©2020 by the Lockman Foundation.

the fullness of all spiritual knowledge takes time, but the basic message is unchanged from what Jesus has spoken. Jesus is the all in all.

Contentment stands out as an authoritative emotional tool the Holy Spirit enables. We sort culture into honorable and dishonorable people and circumstances with our intellect. However, the condition of contentment resting on the truth of God within our hearts is emotional strength. With such strength, we resist culture's shaping force on our humanity. Culture reflects the fullness of temptations that Jesus faced in the wilderness. The world tempts us to seek pleasure for the body, the gain of power, wealth, and fame within the economic and political systems, or to consider ourselves as significant enough that God owes us something (Matt 4:1–11). The key to being content is trusting God for our physical needs, exercising our talents and skills for God's glory, and accepting our humanity with humility. In contentment, we accept enough as better than more.

Contentment builds from learning the spiritual truths revealed in Scripture. In the Gospel of John, Jesus instructs all believers to learn the abiding in him (John 15:1–11). The absolute key to embracing contentment, far greater than any cultural experience in life, is learning the spiritual state of abiding in the Spirit of Christ. By focusing on the Presence of God within us, we discover in him a buffer against the power of our emotions. Engaging the Presence of God as that buffer is the purposeful entry into a spiritual state of resting in one's emotions. This discussion uses intellectual constructs in describing an actual emotional practice at the core of the biblical phrasing, "abiding in Jesus."

Listen to your conscience, especially when it brings to mind anything Jesus has spoken. Act on the guidance of those words, move in that direction, and the sense of God's Presence within deepens. Hearing and obeying the conscience, informed by the written Word and enabled by the Holy Spirit, is the best path. Ignoring one's conscience can cause it to weaken. Habitually ignoring one's conscience leads to silencing a major component of inner identity. A silent conscience is a pitiable state for a human and results in painful consequences.

Beyond issues of conscience, an experience of contentment is often challenged by stress. Under the duress of emotional pressures created by threats of any kind, many people will tell themselves, "It will be okay," as a modulating activity to reduce the emotional storm. For the believer, the in-the-spirit practice to calm one's emotions might be saying aloud, "I trust

You, Jesus," offering simple mental prayers, or reciting Scripture selected in the moment.

There are no specific rules here. Individual experiences may vary. The practice of abiding is the employment of sincere trust in the goodness of God. There is an emotional supply of power in the knowledge of how to maintain one's focus on the Presence of God within, which fulfills the soul and brings wisdom to bear on decision-making. Satisfied peace and contentment result from authentic abiding.

D is for Defying Death
Dissipation, Dependency, Death

THIRTY-FOUR YEARS OF MIDDLE school teaching helped me develop insight into people growing from youths into adults. In open-class discussions, the students occasionally asked questions that philosophers have pondered for ages. Having fun and individual happiness were frequently espoused as basic by students in social studies when topics focused on rights, responsibilities, and privileges within a culture.

Who doesn't like to have fun? Camping, snowboarding, a great movie, friends on a hike, a ride in a convertible—the list is pages long. Experiences for having fun abound. Enjoying them is not wrong. Yet, living simply for the next fun experience opens the disaster door. The word for it is hedonism, or the idea that pleasure has intrinsic value.[1] Though fun activities invite us to feel engaged, excited, and entertained, a life built on seeking fulfillment through whatever "feels good" is a trap for the soul. That trap has a label: dissipation.[2]

Dissipation generally refers to the excessive drinking of alcohol. As teenagers, you will likely be offered drugs or alcohol as a means to have more fun. Some of these substances are legal for adults, while others are illegal. For individuals under the age of twenty-one, all of these substances are illegal in most states. Additionally, be aware that serious harm can result from taking prescription drugs for recreational purposes rather than as prescribed by a doctor. Prescription drugs are safe only when taken under a doctor's supervision.

The pursuit of getting high from "party" substances is often justified solely by the desire to have fun. Knowing people, even family members, who

---

1. Merriam-Webster, *hedonism*, 538.
2. Merriam-Webster, *dissipation*, 336.

consume alcohol in moderation does not justify the use of mind-altering substances as a means of seeking thrills or grabbing for affirmation from peers. It may be tempting to think that consuming substances for increased fun is what adults do. The truth is that immature and maladjusted individuals in chronologically adult human bodies abuse chemical substances.

Discussing the introduction of substances into the body is a vital conversation to have with your parents. If your parents have not spoken to you about alcohol and other party substances, put this book down and ask them to discuss it with you. This is an understanding that you need to have. If another person offers you any substance to ingest, either as a gift or for purchase, red lights need to flash in your head, accompanied by your brain yelling, "Warning! Warning!"

The use of chemical stimulants or depressants for partying is often rationalized as a means of stress relief. There is a wide variety of healthy activities that help relieve stress. Engaging in exercise, quiet time, hobbies, or immersing yourself in comforting environments like forests are excellent activities for processing unpleasant, confusing, or difficult emotions. Chemicals to accomplish the same are a first step toward substance abuse. Substance abuse is the door to addictions.

Addictions are not developed simply by the first use of alcohol, cannabis, or drugs. However, every clear-thinking adult understands that many decisions have unpredictable consequences. First use may develop into a habit. The point at which the habit becomes an actual chemical addiction is reached without realizing the boundary has been crossed. Addiction is often labeled as an illness, yet such conditions begin with a decision, not from infection by a physiological germ.

Consider the significance that our inner being often links emotions, imagination, and desire. The mixture stimulates misjudgment of the physical world in which we bodily exist. Anyone can make unhealthy, unwise decisions due to misjudgments. Misguided decision-making is rife with negative consequences. Psychologically, humans have an innate ability to blind themselves from hurts and dark desires that spur sudden irrational decisions. The Bible teaches about humanity's fall from our created state and describes the consequential "desperately sick heart" (Jer 17:5–10). We are born without the light of the Lord of the Universe in our hearts, and that lack leads to emotional and intellectual malfunction rooted in fear and pride. Dissipation is a consequence of unwisely labeling drunken or chemically altered mental experiences as "fun."

Deep within us, buried beneath what our brains tell us we are feeling, is a motive force. It is the place where emotional needs and intellectual processing intertwine and determine actions seeking fulfillment. Psychologists label this our psyche, defined as " . . . the unique, subjective experience of being in the world."[3] Those not trained in psychology may label these deep forces as functions of the soul. In *Regeneration in Jesus 101*, the term used is "the heart." Biblical wisdom frequently centers on discussions of the heart when giving instruction about understanding our inner reality.

Discerning what is the wisdom from God versus what is the call of the wild around us is an ability gained from being born of God's Spirit. As we employ an ever-broadening spiritual insight, we look inward and evaluate many emotional aspects of the self, especially one's motives.

Determining one's motives is critical to understanding personal behavior. The natural human in the biblical sense is driven by two primary motives: self-preservation and self-satisfaction. These two innate motives are generated by our sense of time. Our natural intellectual reasoning forms within the constraints of the body's limited lifespan. From the onset of puberty, we develop self-consciousness. During adolescence, that self-consciousness is willing to experiment with many experiences searching for personal parameters. All humans experience wanting physical, emotional, and intellectual satisfaction.

Decisions intended to extend one's boundaries are ordered, for better or worse, by the defining forces of our natural motives working within physical reality. Our natural state has two primary yet opposing motivations: to avoid death and to seek satisfaction through acquisition. As we enter adulthood, those motivations become more potent as each confronts the limits of time lived. Death then means being unfulfilled within the limited time available, and satisfaction means the pride we experience from acquiring wealth or fame.

Fear of death is sometimes called the "mother of all fears." Many fears place impractical constraints on emotional and intellectual processes and reduce one's best abilities to think critically. Facing death, even just seriously considering dying, reaches deeply into the meaning of existence and whether or not there is an eternal reality.

Extreme sports are entertainment activities often labeled as "death-defying." Rock climbing without gear is an example. An activity with a life-threatening component provides a powerful adrenaline rush. The

---

3. Merriam-Webster, *psyche*, 942

participant must manage emotions to remain unperturbed by the danger faced. Proficiency in such fear management is the key to success in extreme sports. Choosing dangerous activities for thrills pushes an individual into deeper levels of self-awareness as a function of overcoming fear. Beyond the emotional growth experience, extreme sports also boost the ego. Earning the admiration and accolades from others feeds one's pride. Earning glory for sporting achievement and attaining an exalted reputation for physical prowess carries the allure of self-attained significance.

Fear of death evaporates once the promise of eternal life is intellectually understood and fully embraced in the heart. Inner peace springs from the spiritual truth that there is a God who is utterly trustworthy. Spirit-life, the connection with the Eternal Being and Creator, is deeply satisfying. Hear this message: the Father desires those born of him to understand life as being a soul guided by the Holy Spirit and passing through a human experience. In contrast, extreme human experiences intended to define the level of depth of one's being do not foster spiritual enlightenment.

The world where we live offers a multitude of distracting, self-satisfying choices across the three faculties of experience: physical, emotional, and intellectual. The distractions exert a counterfeit power, an excitement known as a function of the body's existence. God intervenes to open our understanding and give us a reality based on him. Realization of connection to God and the prospect of eternity with the Father frees the individual from a need to seek the ultimate anything: an ultimate high induced by chemicals, the ultimate material success, or the ultimate thrill.

The protection we need from ourselves is fundamental: seek the wisdom of the Lord. A Christian develops values built on the understanding of God revealed in the Bible and practices commensurate decision-making. Learn the strength of heart brought by his Spirit to your inner being. Inner strength from the Spirit of Christ grows by leaving behind false views of life for the intentional pursuit of maturing in spirit. We all face the end of the physical body; we all will physically die. The end of the physical body marks the soul's transition to the next level of existence. In the meantime, seek spiritual understanding above all motivations rooted in self-absorption.

E is for Evergreen
Evil, Economics, Eternity

A SIXTEEN-YEAR-OLD IS ALMOST an adult. An eighteen-year-old is considered a legal adult with rights, more privileges, and considerably more responsibilities. Eighteen years opens the culture-based opportunity to enlist in the military, but purchasing alcoholic beverages or renting a car is prohibited until more years have been lived. The more significant issue is the maturity manifested by an individual. While some may be old enough to purchase alcohol, they often lack the maturity to consume it responsibly.

Contemplating one's future is a common experience for teenagers around the world. The best decisions stand on solid values, not on dreams of acquired wealth or sentimentalized emotional satisfaction. Recognize that you are more than just a mind and body with a future in the material world. Instead, embrace a perspective of the individual as mind, body, and an immortal soul. Scripture validates the eternity of the soul. This foundational perspective on life strengthens one's ability to confront personal obstacles, the seeming randomness of life events, and the grievous inhumanities that people commit against one another.

The inhumanity stems from the overall human deficit: the lack of compassion. The take-advantage-of-others mindset roots in the human heart with startling similarities across cultures and periods. Envy, pride, deceit, fornication, and alarming levels of violence are compelling evidence that God exists. The revealed truth in the Bible warns that mayhem is the fruit of being separated from God (Gal 5:19–21). People often decry Christian views of God, asking, "If there is a God, how could he allow all this horrible inhumanity to exist?" The answer is simple: Human selfishness is observable and affirms that God gives humans free will choice.

E is for Evergreen

The fall of humanity from the peace-filled intent of God for his creation and the need for the intervention of Jesus as the Savior of humanity is a function of human free will. The basic biblical narrative is that God created humans; humans rejected him, which results in evil entering the human experience; and God intervened through his Son, Jesus Christ, to reverse the effects of the rebellion. When we witness murder, hatred, rape, greed, and similar acts, we are observing humans under the influence of the "god of this world," the adversarial entity leading a rebellion against the true Lord of Earth.

Societal discord across the planet often boils down to economics. Economics is the system developed over millennia that enables the acquisition of one's needs and wants. Competition over natural resources undermines the dominion that God intended for humans to exercise over the ground, water, and air. If compassion rather than competition governed the development and distribution of Earth's resources, the bounty would supply all needs. Aggressive competition is further evidence of a god of this world luring humans into grievous selfishness. This statement is not an advertisement for communal communism. All human economic systems will fail as long as humanity rejects the authority of God.

If greed corrupts the economics underlying the global market, it is also evident that greed corrupts the political systems linked to economics. Human productivity is the driving force behind resource utilization and wealth development. Governments harness human productivity through taxation and other means. We willingly accept government rule because stable societies require the rule of law to maintain order. Government taxation is justified as a means of ensuring human welfare. This justification sounds noble. In practice, greed transforms governments into using humans as wealth-generating power sources. This tension between the need for government and being victimized by government is one of the dynamics driving our cultural divide in the United States. Arguments continually arise over how the money generated by taxation will be spent. Who benefits and why from the common till we all produce?

Given the corrupting effect of greed on those who gain power, humans cannot create a better world on their own. Yet, it is inspiring to hope we might create a better world. There are people in all cultures willing to sacrifice much to benefit humanity and hope that a better world emerges. These motivated people do much good, but at some point, compromise and corruption taint the best of intentions. "Doing good" is defined by the world around us as the attainment of peace, prosperity, and safety for humans. It is a siren's song, an often used mantra of the politician, the rich, the famous, and grassroots efforts to achieve social justice. Look closely, and you will find within this list many voices who reject Jesus Christ. Many who seek to do good have rejected Christ.

Am I saying we do not need to bother with doing good deeds? Not at all. The good we do springs from spiritual oneness with our Lord, the Father-Son-Holy Spirit. Jesus stirs us to work for good in his name (Titus 2:14).[1] He calls us to relieve suffering, give encouragement, and lend our support to others, particularly other Christians in need. In this technological age, we find ourselves confronted by global human needs. Christians seek to be the feet, the mouth, and the hands of God's will in loving others. However, we will not change the whole world nor remove the pain driven by the sinful rebellion against God. We wait longingly for God's reign over the earth to be restored.

Since the Bible instructs Christians to submit to secular governance, we consequently submit to a tumultuous status quo of corrupt earthly power over our bodies (Rom 13:1). Yet, we embrace an eternal King ruling our hearts. We confront a dynamic tension between our King's reign over our hearts and the governance of other humans over our productivity. This is our state as Christians: we know we are citizens of a higher kingdom while we endure human governance exacted in opposition to God. It will be so until Jesus returns and establishes direct rule over the earth.

Our best response is conforming to the truth that we are born of God's Spirit, and thereby confirm we are his creation while we live among vast numbers of people in rebellion against the Creator. With our inner eyes opened by our second birth, we rely on God and seek his purposes for us. We experience a profound paradigm shift of meaning and purpose. We have real hope in the eternal plan of our Father and know a solid peace in the midst of the mayhem generated by the rebellion against God.

Living in the spirit of God is akin to being an evergreen tree. We are a distinct type of human due to the Presence of the Lord. We are fully a "tree" like everyone else, but those whose human experience is dominated by pride, fear, and selfishness are dormant deciduous trees. Those without God's Spirit are the bare branches of humanity. The Holy Spirit of God

---

1. Paraphrases adapted from the New American Standard Bible: ©2020 by the Lockman Foundation.

is given to us in the born-again experience. We are vibrant and full of life while living among the dormancy of those blinded by the false god of this world. The wonderful truth is that anyone can leave dormancy and become an evergreen tree. It is the Father's desire for all to be joined to him (Titus 2:11).

F is for Flying Free
Feelings, Fear, Freedom

I HAVE BEEN A student who later became a teacher. I have experienced educational challenges just as my students have. I have created challenges for my students. I observed two key factors that ensure success at any stage of life: workload management and appropriate interpersonal relationships. Be prepared—the adult work world expects much more responsibility than school ever did. Interaction with other adults will also be more complicated. Developing positive feelings and habits toward work and people during your school years supports a smooth transition into adulthood.

Everyone experiences the waxing and waning of positive and negative feelings in response to their immediate circumstances. Relational, cultural, and environmental external sources, interpreted through one's perceptions shaped by past experiences, stir the emotional well-being within us. A positive perception of current circumstances will resonate within us, and a negative perception will perturb us. Illustrating this line of thought are the fears we experience during any given day. An adult might fear strange dogs but have no recollection of the dog bite received while a toddler.

We are all wired to experience fear on different levels. A stark difference exists between an identified threat of a storm that spurs an action of seeking shelter and a sudden loud, unidentifiable bang seizing the emotions in a frenzy of panic. Basic fears often impose unwarranted limits on decision-making and behavior. Compounding the problem is fear based on misconceptions, unfounded presumptions, or simply wrong information. When fear underlies and drives our feelings, we become vulnerable to costly mistakes.

Beyond fears, humans experience extreme feelings of being invigorated or despondent, hopeful or wary, determined or reluctant, and more.

Our spontaneous reactions and deliberate choices of action can result from nothing more than a feeling. However, feelings are usually not a reliable evaluation tool. This unreliability is particularly evident when our feelings arise from fear.

Strong feelings are clearly rooted in psychological needs, such as the desire to be loved or to love another. The science of psychology offers multiple organizing frameworks for understanding our deep needs. Here is a framework proposed by researcher Klaus Grawe. He identifies four basic needs: the need for attachment; the need for control/orientation; the need for self-enhancement; and the need for pleasure/avoidance of pain.[1]

Another factor shaping our feelings is physiological, that is, behavior based on meeting physical needs. Consider more basic drives, such as the need for shelter, food, clothing, and our biological drive to procreate. The choices anyone makes, whether building a future destiny or engaging in momentary frivolity, result from a goal of fulfilling a perceived need. These needs may be psychological, physiological, or a combination of the two.

The challenge we each face as adults is developing effective strategies for success in the material world that satisfy our deep emotional and physical drives. Our basic psychological needs and the complexity of interacting with other people may lead to strong yet confusing feelings. Experiencing fear amid this complexity is not uncommon. Most people understand fear as a psychological condition.

Framed in the context of this book, fear is also a spiritual experience. Each of the four needs comes with potential fears: loss of attachment with a significant object of one's affection (people, animals); loss of structure on which is built a sense of security; fear that we are inadequate (especially felt as a young adult); pleasure lost or painful circumstances encountered. A Christian has the opportunity to experience the fear of these losses and resist, through the spirit, any incumbent burden fear might foment.

Humans have a goal or a reason for any behavior. Fears may be an unidentified motivator of personal reasoning or goal setting. Our self-awareness of any given fear may not have cognitively developed, and the fear remains neither named nor understood. For example, the fear of experiencing poverty may motivate striving to succeed, but the striving individual regards the motive as determination. Unrecognized fear is a negative influence on sound decision-making.

---

1. Grawe, *Neuropsychotherapy*, 171.

People often explain and justify actions rooted in feelings as an issue of personal expression of identity. People will rationalize a habit or learned behavior as a personality characteristic. Some will exhibit harmful or antisocial behavior patterns and explain them as, "That's just the way I am." In this expression, people intend to deflect challenges against their irrational personal choices. Maturing as a person occurs as we learn to recognize our inner motivations. Equipped with that recognition, the obvious growth point is to assume responsibility and practice effective management of personal feelings and fears.

The good news is that none of us actually must discipline sinfulness away or master fears. Before explaining a better way, adjust the frame of reference by substituting the word *selfishness* for *sinfulness*. Selfishness blocks our ability to love others and is at the root of our resistance to obeying God. Selfishness is fertile emotional soil for fear or other negative feelings to grow and control us.

God the Father calls us through Jesus, the Son, to recognize that perfect love casts out fear! Fear is relieved by the truth of God. Finding fulfillment of our four psychological needs and relief from associated fear is completely opened to us in the born-again paradigm. Jesus is called "the life" in John 1:3. He demonstrated the emotional framework of a different level of humanity. The born-again experience allows the substance, the spirit, of Jesus's level of humanity to be placed within us. A new heart and emotional framework are given as an act of grace from the Father. The Scripture teaches us to set aside our old feelings and fears by considering them dead, and to put on the new feelings (Rom 6:11; Col 3:9–10).[2] We live beyond the fear in our new spirit being.

The power of Jesus's words, "The truth shall set you free," unfolds. Due to a literal new spirit, one's heart has the potential to mature fully as a human. We grow equipped with a new mechanism for understanding psychological needs and a newfound power of choice against our selfishness. Knowing one possesses the power to choose obedience over sinful temptations is a part of the abundant life promised to the regenerated human (Eph 3:20).

Culturally and collectively, humans often reduce the meaning of freedom to the belief that one can do anything as long as others are not harmed. The siren's call within culture cries out for the freedom to "be me."

---

2. Paraphrases adapted from the New American Standard Bible: ©2020 by the Lockman Foundation.

In the United States, people expect, demand, and seek the freedom to make personal decisions and determine personal destiny. However, individual choice is often used as a license for much behavior God calls sin. In effect, people desire selfishly and demand the freedom to live within the fallen nature.

Ironically, humans are bound by sinful feelings and robbed of the true freedom they seek: the power to choose. Jesus taught that the person who commits sin is a slave to sin (John 8:34). A more satisfying human experience and a more substantive humanity occur when any person rises above selfishness and fear. True freedom is obtained when we confront the God of the Bible and choose his plan, his truth, and his goodness.

Walking with God by following the teachings in the two testaments of the Bible lifts the believer into true freedom. True freedom is not merely doing as one pleases. The Earth now groans under the weight of selfishness resulting from the choice to live as we please (Rom 8:19). The pride, fear, greed, and lust of humans cause much of the pain we see around us now: hatred and its murders, lust and its rapes, greed and its injustice. Understanding freedom, as delineated by Jesus in the statement, "The truth shall set you free," is understanding the power to stand against one's own selfishness. True freedom comes in submitting to the Spirit of God.

Want a better world? Be a wholesome person separated from the greed and lust of this age. Walking in his Spirit releases our inner being to choose the virtue of serving others. The regenerated person lives and moves in God. We know our greatest reality and freedom by developing spirit awareness. The ups and downs of our feelings, sorted through the guidance of the Holy Spirit, stimulate a deeper understanding of life above and beyond the material existence of the body. The spiritual freedom won for us by Jesus is a supreme sense of adventure and wonder.

"Walking in the spirit" is a common phrase used in Christian circles. The phrase "walk in the spirit" is found in Scripture (Rom 8:4). Also, authors across the spectrum of historical Christianity describe varied experiences related to the precept of "abiding in Christ," which is a direct instruction from Jesus (John 15:1–11). The vine-abiding principle is described by authors from across the spectrum of Christian experience throughout history who all speak clearly of this dynamic practice.

Flying is a fair metaphor. The inner world, the intangible person we are, lifts out of the mire of confusion and conflict we sometimes feel in reaction to the material world around us. By our volition, we rest in the Spirit of

God, and our inner person rides on the wings of truth. We move above the negative feelings of selfishness, fear, revenge, jealousy, and envy; we fly into the pure air of God's goodness, freed from selfishness and able to embrace compassion, kindness, humility, and contentment.

I write the words of this book to stir you to seek and live, standing on the spiritual work of Jesus on the cross and in the power of his resurrection. His Holy Spirit will equip anyone to live spirit-filled, the intent of God since creation.

G is for Guidance through the Gauntlet
Greed, Guilt, Gratitude

THE BIBLE IS CONSIDERED by Christians to be the written word of God. How are words compiled within an ancient context so pointedly applicable to the twenty-first century? The content of the Bible, and in particular the New Testament, enlivens the emotions, challenges the intellectual constructs about material existence, and capably guides an individual into new spiritual territory. The substance of basic instruction on living life knowing God can be grasped and practiced. The words are inherently transformative. Once Jesus is accepted as God in the flesh, the work ahead of the believer is the maturation of the new person born again in spirit.

God's plan is entered by individual choice, but without other humans, God's plan for any individual remains unfulfilled. God's plan for humans is maturation in the love that fills heaven. We need other humans to learn love as determined by the Lord. The gathering of believers is a fellowship classroom. Accepting the need for Christian fellowship raises the question, "What constitutes a healthy, holy, and hospitable church group?" Congregations that focus on impure motives or misguided goals may exist. Avoid them. What characterizes an unhealthy group? To answer that question, several broad principles need consideration.

Think about greed. The billions of people worldwide are all capable of greed. The clear evidence that a person loves gaining more stuff is easily spotted. The Bible reveals the wisdom needed to navigate life, and it teaches that the love of wealth is the root cause of evil among humans.

Wealth is not evil. A person of relatively small income can be a greedy person. The issue isn't how much money anyone has acquired, but whether gaining more money is the desire of one's heart. For a Christian living in a society built around wealth acquisition, there is a dynamic tension between acquiring money and not loving its power. In Christian life, prioritizing wealth gain to impress others indicates a weak, weakening, or lost love for God. Greed is an emotional state locked on the notion that wealth is of prime importance. It wrecks a person's faith.

Can a church be greedy? A church group can walk in falsehood, just as an individual can. Money and its use are ways to discern the difference between the practice of Christian religion and a sincere walk of faith. I walk a fine line here. I do not want to judge anyone or any group improperly. Anyone claiming Christ answers to the Lord alone. Nonetheless, be discerning about the experiences a church offers and sensitive to group attitudinal errors (Matt 10:15–16).[1] One key tool for discerning something amiss is an examination of the money decisions of the leadership.

A majority of churches offer sincere leadership seeking to serve the spiritual needs of the congregation, spread the message of the Gospel of Jesus, and care for hurting people. Unfortunately, wayward groups use enticements and guilt-generating tactics to increase giving. It may be subtle, but it is relatively easy to spot. Giving is your choice and reflects joy in the Lord. When you feel shamed, compelled, or coerced to give to a particular ministry, look carefully at what is happening.

The reality is that some pastors are wolves in sheep's clothing, as the Scripture says. Jesus calls them hirelings in John, chapter 10. Success for these pastors is not measured by the spiritual maturing of congregants, but instead is calculated from a personal gain in material wealth. An emphasis on growth is often a part of stated missions. What is the heart behind the outreach to others? Look at this carefully. Sermons heaping guilt on members for failure to witness often reveal the problem.

Condemnation by a leader—pastor, elder, deacon, or a church teacher—for lack of Christian virtue or lack of works is not Christian faith. Attitudes of self-righteousness by a group or leadership reveal the lack of the Spirit of Jesus.

A gauntlet of challenges faces young Christians becoming adults and new converts of any age. First are challenges spawned by the selfish old nature—motivations and ideas centered on self-enhancement or gaining pleasure particularly. Also, false guidance lurks behind various emotional manipulations intent on using believers as income. Finally, the larger culture around us offers a myriad of distractions that only provide counterfeits

---

1. Paraphrases adapted from the New American Standard Bible: ©2020 by the Lockman Foundation.

G is for Guidance through the Gauntlet

of inner satisfaction, keeping us away from the inner being's needed nourishment from God's Spirit.

How do you strengthen your spiritual self against false Christian teaching and the allure of all that is against God? Read the Bible, yes; but study it, as well. Reckon with, reflect on, and seek to walk in the truth written there. Always remember, it is not about proving your point or having a Scripture to stand on; instead, the goal is to know abiding in Jesus's Spirit as a real practice. He guides the mind to understand, and his nature steadies our emotions. Read the words of Jesus often.

Learning to walk in the Spirit of the Lord is not some spooky connection with the spirit world requiring trances or suffering as a lifestyle. As a young believer, there is a simple starting point. If greed is the root of all evil, gratitude is the opposite. Gratitude is a practical choice that opens the door to understanding the worship of the one True God. The often repeated phrase, "Count your blessings," is not just a sweet platitude of optimism. Instruction from both the Old and New Testament includes gratitude. It is a load-bearing pillar of the inner person, an emotional state that opens a human to the guiding hand of the Holy Spirit.

When do you need to express gratitude to the Lord God? That is the easiest part of this. Whenever you hear yourself complaining, STOP. Listen with self-awareness for complaints in your stream of consciousness. STOP thinking complaints as well. Recognize when feelings empathize with complaints generated by a friend and STOP. After each stop, acknowledge the goodness of God and offer thanks. Replace the old pattern with a new one. This is a spiritual discipline.

The spirit-life revealed by Jesus is the path to pursue in this life. Abiding and resting in his Holy Spirit is *the way* of life (John 14:6). Learning gratitude is an active, real-time exercise in developing an overall sense of the indwelling Holy Spirit as the spiritual state that God intends for those who know him.

The developed cultures of humanity, the emotional interactions of humans, and one's labyrinth of emotional states are significant categories of powerful obstacles adults face in managing life. There is pressure to conform and expectations to be cool by non-conformity. There is pressure to earn a living or to perform well for causes. The gauntlet of false perspectives counterfeiting a life well-lived is long and broad. Some even claim to be Christian.

Spirit-life is the inner breathing of our being. As a Christian, we breathe in Jesus's nature as it is revealed in the God-breathed, 2,000 year-old Bible. He enlightens our thinking, strengthens our character, and comforts our hearts. In the spirit-life formed by the Lord, he is the Author and Perfecter of faith (Heb 12:2). Thus, we walk free of greed and guilt ruling over our reactions and responsive choices. We live as he intended for us in the creation. He is working to regenerate humanity one born-again identity at a time. As a person born of the Spirit and on the maturation journey, embrace gratitude for communion with God.

H is for the Heart
Humanism, Hubris, Humility

Humanism, a challenging word to corral, has two historical meanings: an original, broader use during the Renaissance in Europe, which included the institutional church; and its modern usage, a secular philosophical approach to humanity distinct from any sacred associations. In both its 600-year-old context and our contemporary one, humanism is what it looks like: focus on humanity; and any *-ism* is a belief or condition. Thus, humanism is a belief about our human condition.

The Renaissance is a major turning point in the historical development of Western Civilization. Scholars across Western Europe during the period studied ancient Greek and Roman literature, which fueled the renewal of European culture. This intellectual renewal movement drove the exploration of new ideas across European cultures. Science, art, architecture, and literature, as well as the institutions of education and religion, emphasized education with a distinct sophistication rooted in classical literature.[1]

The early Renaissance expression of Christianity, the Catholic Church, shifted its understanding and application of the Bible. Humanism emerged as a philosophical proposition within church scholarship efforts. The term conveyed the idea that humanity benefited from scholarship based on how ideas were researched and expressed.[2] The essence, then, of a renewed interest in learning from antiquity had both a sacred and a secular context.

The invention of the Gutenberg printing press spurred communication and facilitated a rapid spread of ideas across the collective Renaissance experience. Johannes Gutenberg essentially laid the rails on which culture would speed into the future like a roaring train. Modernity formed and

1. McGrath, *Christian Theology*, 40.
2. McGrath, *Christian Theology*, 40.

leaped forward on knowledge proliferating within and distributed through books. Intellectual and literary explorations, as well as growing scientific and technological discoveries, challenged the political and religious institutions of the period. The roots of the Modern Era reach deeply into Renaissance scholarship.

Humanism has evolved in meaning since its first appearance as an exploratory term during the Renaissance. While the wording may vary from one writer to another, humanism is now summarized as the view that humans rely on reason, logic, and naturalism, rather than religious dogma and supernaturalism.[3] Much of the philosophical orientation of the term since the twentieth century is the dichotomy between those who believe in God and those who do not.

Unpacking that a bit, humanism altered its meaning in the Modern Era, evolving into the idea that humans use intellect, logic, and emotional caring to determine the best course without expectations or supervision by any deity. Many atheists camp here, but a person can believe in the modern definition of humanism and be an agnostic as well.

Ironically, don't be surprised if a person attends religion-based events as a function of family heritage or is committed to positive thinking or transcendental meditation and also expresses humanism as their guiding principle. There is a stark contrast, however, between humanism and belief in God's order for humanity. It is the contrast in perspectives on the human spirit. Consider *spirit* as the truth on which human consciousness establishes individual meaning and finds trustworthy guidance. Humanism believes in the individual and society, the human collective, as the only sources of truth. The Bible teaches that humans can find guidance into goodness only through the Spirit of God as the source of truth.

Humanism trusts natural humans as capable of individual goodness, who thereby establish a just society. Jesus points to an authority wiser than humanity as the source of goodness, which calls humanity to love one another. Paul calls the "natural" person the problem (1 Cor 2:14). Being a natural man or woman does not mean a lack of intellectual seeking of societal order or that the emotional heart lacks a desire for peace among people. The biblical view is that a natural person is self-centered and thus continually in conflict with others.

The humanist credo illustrates the separation between religion and faith. Humanists view the imperatives and restrictions on human behavior

---

3. Grudin, "humanism."

ascribed to deity as meaningless words. Humanism asserts that any deified moral standards cannot be true. From the humanist or naturalist philosophical perspective, religions teach human conjectures about a non-existent supernatural realm.

Why live according to somebody's human extrapolations regarding an unprovable supernaturalism? The humanist's incredulity regarding religion is easily understood. Why indeed? Where is the wisdom in trusting something that does not exist? Religions exist because humans need to explain what cannot be seen and is hoped to exist. Do religions hold no wisdom? If something is false, it cannot be true or wise.

Under the label of Christianity, some congregations meet, discuss, and hear sermons built around references to a supernatural God as specified in the Bible. The event of gathering stems from historical practices of specific rituals and traditions of the group. The power of God is often denied or overlooked. Participants in religion regard it as a duty to experience the ritual, but may find themselves doubting God's love and faithfulness (2 Tim 3:1–5).[4]

Stated another way, a practitioner of religious forms states a belief in a supernatural god but does not search for understanding in the Scripture or in prayer and meditation. Seeking wisdom instead through secular self-help books, these folks trust in human logic, unbelieving of connecting with the indwelling Holy Spirit. This represents a dilemma of expressing beliefs about the words, rather than embodying what is known through living the words. If a congregant in a church group (no matter the religion label above the door) is not supported through instruction and encouragement to participate in the supernatural, regenerated spirit life lived through knowledge of the indwelling Holy Spirit of Jesus, something is amiss.

One can own a bicycle, read about the principles of riding it, imagine riding it, and discuss it with others, but actual practice on the bicycle is essential to learning how to ride. Only developed skill enables the exhilaration of riding downhill, and only discipline equips one with the power to pedal uphill. Understanding the ways of the Spirit of the Lord requires a singular focus on him and results in a daily personal practice of abiding in him.

The complicated thing to recognize is that human pride and arrogance can often be expressed through the use of Christian idioms and language. The pastor, a group of leaders, or the entire congregation can embrace pride

---

4. Paraphrases adapted from the New American Standard Bible: ©2020 by the Lockman Foundation.

in defining religious dogma. However, a dogmatic emphasis driven by pride is a path to spiritual death, not true life.

In contrast with dogmatic teaching and traditions of ritual, Christians gather to support one another in learning the ways of spirit-life. Functioning Christian spirit-life opens the door to thinking *and* feeling as instructed by the New Testament record of Jesus and the Apostles. Christian faith is the embrace of the Holy Spirit and produces profound results. God has opened our understanding of our non-material reality. The non-material state, consciousness of our spirit existence, matures through disciplined effort over time. An individual also chooses a group with whom to share the processes of spiritual growth. We are all shaped for better or worse as a function of our group associations.

A group experience of an attitude of humility before God is a powerful reinforcement for individual growth in the ways of God. A primary responsibility of a supplicant to God is the personal development of humility. A group of people sharing humble devotion before God and practicing the application of spirit-life imperatives is also God's intention. The development of individual godliness supports building a society of people who know how to love one another. This is a church. A church of believers actively living out Christian society reveals the glory of our Lord Jesus to the natural people observing.

A shared attitude of pride, apathy, or any other negative feeling reduces the understanding of God. Attitudes are a manifestation of the spirit within. This dynamic is among the reasons people today reject Christianity as the truth. When church arrogance masquerades as piety, only those deceived by the costume believe that what is being said and done is the truth.

The common use of the word *amazing* in today's culture illustrates a lack of understanding our God and the human condition. When we examine ourselves within the material realm, it is popular these days to see the basic human as "amazing." We have skills, talents, and intelligence. In well-functioning teams, there is tremendous accomplishment. Consequently, humans collectively are "amazing." The truth is that God is amazing, and his creation of humans proves it! This is the fruit of humanism: we want the glory attributed to us without any acknowledgment of God.

Cultural beauty standards add a harmful layer of meaning to the use of *amazing* as a modifier. Celebrating appearance is arbitrary, fleeting, and entirely based on only one human facet: the body. We have unleashed many harmful emotional traps for individuals by exalting a developed human body and the manner of adornment style in its presentation.

Appearance, intelligence, talent, and skills are all temporary conditions based on the material body. That body will age and die. No material attributes matter beyond death. People have recorded evidence of individual physical existence, such as video clips, print, audio recordings, and writings of notable achievements and related notoriety. A few generations pass, and only researchers ever see the records of our existence. Most of us leave little trace that we existed. Our body's presence on earth is remembered only as long as someone who knew us has a memory.

What truly matters is our spiritual state, the emotional matrix of one's identity. Are we compassionate or uncaring, gentle or brutal, serving or dominating, insightful into truth or blind to it, acting with humility or brazen in hubris? As natural humans, we either think of ourselves as amazing due to something material, or we experience feelings of inferiority, believing we fail the amazing test.

Due to negativity, fear, selfishness, or pride controlling us from within, we all run headlong at some point into hard consequences. Some poor souls are conquered by addictions; many live in conflict with another person's will or in a constant fight for a piece of the money pie, or both; some end up alone and without true friends. The list of consequences for being ruled by the negative traits of a natural human is long.

Real-life consequences spring from a person's spiritual, the inner being, state. This connection between the inner state governing choices and the resulting consequences is the fundamental reason psychiatry exists, is it not? Why humans behave as they do is a question that both atheists and theists ask. Science analyzes the psyche and offers therapies of drugs, counseling, and the development of logical coping mechanisms to gain a sense of identity without the negative emotion. Scripture names one's heart condition (psyche) as the problem and offers an exchange of the natural human emotional matrix for the heart God intended in the beginning.[5]

Consider the difference between mass and weight, and similarly differentiate human substance, the soul, and the pull on that substance as

---

5. I do not imply that professional help is unhelpful or wrong. When behavior is out of control, material solutions such as drug therapies or group support systems may serve the purpose of stopping self-destructive behaviors. Material ways of reversing a harmful lack of self-control may be part of a personal journey. However, these interventions do not address the root problem of the inherently selfish nature with which we are all born. Only being born of the spirit begins the new life paradigm.

spirit. The soul exists eternally, but the spirit held in the heart is the rudder by which decisions in this life are guided. We all yearn for our souls to be fed and nourished through meaning and purpose. If the spirit connection to God remains in its natural, disconnected state, we seek the soul's sustenance in the counterfeit of thrills, blindness to goodness, and moral lies spewing from the spirit of Lucifer, the Antichrist. Human souls consuming the false remain starved, thirsting, and spiritually naked (Rev 3:17).

The first step and the journey of the Christian spirit-life ride on the choice of humility. Spirit birth begins in humility before the Father, as a person acknowledges that selfishness is one's core reality and the need is great for being saved from our human nature. Humility accepts the gift of God's grace, making a way to know him through the spiritual work of Jesus, the Conqueror of sin and death. Growth as a spirit person occurs through the Spirit of the Lord within the heart. Hearing his Presence and obeying the Spirit are the spiritual functions that settle our eternal soul's sense of well-being into peace with God.

The absolute truth is God's holiness, lovingkindness, and grace. Nothing we do has any impact on God's prerogatives as Creator nor his initiated reach for redeeming humanity through the Atonement of Jesus's self-sacrifice. On this side of heaven, however, human responsibility is a key component in the embrace of God's rich, rewarding spirit-life. We exercise the God-given power of free will when we decide to submit to God. We exercise free will when we decide to seek understanding and apply the consequential knowledge to being focused on the spiritual light, the Presence of the Holy Spirit.

A person in the spirit of Jesus is equipped for the life God intended for his creation. Living in communion with the Holy Spirit is a life of impact. It begins as God's grace opens us to the new birth. The choice of humility in the heart to receive his gift, opens the path to eternity. Yet, an individual's maturing into the likeness of Jesus is a function of seeking maturity, an act of one's free will. Humility or hubris is a personal choice with life-determining consequences. Receiving grace to be born again results from humility before God. Walking in grace is living in humility, like that of a dependent child. Christian faith becomes a daily exercise of the will to be in him.

I is for Illumination
Idolatry, Insecurity, Intimacy

ON FEBRUARY 9, 1964, the Beatles first appeared on U.S. television sets.[1] I sat in front of our family TV, a black-and-white model. My mom, older siblings, and I witnessed the Fab Four's debut in the United States with about forty percent of the U.S. population.[2] I was only eight, but I understood the excitement I saw on television.

I vividly remember the news film clips showing crowds of screaming teenage girls meeting the band at the airport, and the Ed Sullivan Show's camera telecasting the same behavior as it panned across the audience. I didn't quite understand the term *idol* heard in the news and conversations of the day, but I learned soon enough. The Beatles were idols to those screaming fans. Young women in the audience gave themselves over to avid devotion.

Idolatry means immoderate attachment or devotion.[3] An idol is an object worshiped as a symbol of something thought to be spiritually powerful. Various statues representing deities idolized during ancient times are housed in museums today. Idolatry continues in today's world. Now, in addition to symbols such as a smiling Buddha statue, living people are also idolized. Film stars, professional athletes, and rock stars gain fans and become idolized celebrities.

Strong identification with a celebrity is not considered practicing idolatry in a biblical sense. However, statues and other objects have historically been idolized in the practice of emotive worship since ancient times to now. In contemporary culture, as the Beatles example illustrates, living humans

1. Smithsonian Institution. "Beatles' First Appearance."
2. Smithsonian Institution. "Beatles' First Appearance."
3. Merriam-Webster, *idolatry*, 576.

frequently receive extreme devotional behavior from others. American culture generates idol-level, avid devotion toward objects that reflect fame, wealth, or status. A middle-aged man may adore (idolize) his red, powerful convertible because of its symbolic message of youth, vigor, accumulated wealth, or all three. In effect, he worships the image of himself enhanced in his mind by owning the sports car.

Hitler understood the use of idols; let's call them symbols of power. He emblazoned the swastika on giant unfurled banners, the national flag, and cast it in metal for adorning the tops of poles and building facades. He intended a reverence among the German populace for Nazi idealism. The swastika inspired the regular citizen to perceive and revere the German state with singular importance. The Nazis pushed national pride to blind devotion for what the *symbol* represented. Symbolic idolatry, which is not religion-based, is an embedded characteristic of the modern era.

Closer to our contemporary time and culture, consider a serialized television contest that seeks and gains a massive audience for new singing talent. The show title says it clearly, *American Idol*. The production airs on television as a platform for the winner to become idolized. Frequently it works! The talented individual winning the competition may actually draw national renown and significant wealth. We make idols out of people rooted in the desire to be famous or rich ourselves.

An influential cultural pull on people is the development of the self as the path to happiness. Throughout advertising, media entertainments, and institutional education, we hear and read references about self-image, self-actualization, the true self, or the authentic self. A person's self-perception is the overall goal, making the self the object of focus. See a problem?

Developing self-image, protecting self-image, and projecting confidence in one's self-image have become core values and desired goals. The basis for aesthetic plastic surgery and some aspects of therapeutic counseling is built on the assumption of the value of a positive self-image. Both plastic surgery and counseling are valuable avenues of intervention when injury to the body or the heart damages the quality of life. The point here is not a critique of the medical community's efforts to help the injured. Instead, the focus is on the developed societal value that one's physical appearance or emotional impact must be protected and, as needed, improved. Self-esteem is sought with determination as the final answer to finding self-satisfaction in one's life.

I is for Illumination

Until about the mid-twentieth century, service to family, community, and the nation under-girded a cultural perspective on how one gains meaning and purpose in life. Now, personal development is touted as the vehicle to meaning. The motivation for one's dedication and effort in life is the self. The self is viewed as the source of all emotional strength.

There is an inevitable chaos visited upon egocentric individuals gathered into groups. A dominant characteristic of current society is the frequency of clashing egos and the consequential chaos that forms around competing self-images. In *The Lord of the Rings* trilogy, Tolkien symbolizes evil as a conical tower with an all-seeing eye floating above the circular parapet. Thus, a lowercase "i" becomes a metaphor for evil. Tolkien metaphorically depicts self-exaltation as evil itself. In contrast, Almighty God says to Moses—and Jesus repeats this in the New Testament—"I Am." God names himself as the eternal and complete entity of being and identity.

Tolkien paints that picture by naming the land where the evil resides "Mordor." This fictional place name sounds like *mortal*, which you will recognize as inevitable death. Mortal derives from Latin *mortalis*, meaning death.[4]

I do not know that Tolkien intended we make this connection of Mordor as selfishness and death. Yet, in my life experience, I know that when selfishness determines my choices, I harm myself and others. I observe this dynamic in the lives of people around me, in recorded history, and in literature from around the globe. The harm caused by selfishness is a central theme across the whole of human experience.

Selfish decisions are the result of belief in a perceived benefit. Living within a search for selfish benefits is a spiritual condition. People are frequently blind to the shortcomings of their character resulting from selfishness. Life experience draws attention to selfish patterns in our character. These patterns will either be justified in our view of ourselves, or we will decide that a change is needed.

Self-awareness electing change indicates an individual identifies a need for maturing in the inner being. The issue then becomes a change in direction. What is a good direction? There are two spirit realities embedded around us: one is good and pure, and one is evil and thus harmful. One of the most critical aspects of the truth revealed through understanding Jesus is that selflessness is the nature of God. God is good and reveals through

---

4. Merriam Webster, *mortal*, 758.

the Son, Jesus, sacrificial love as the bedrock of all goodness. Whatever is against God in us traverses the thought stream as me-first priorities and reflects the old nature in the heart.

We are a three-part person: the body is our tent temporarily giving us a place to dwell; the mind generates the words of conscious understanding, and thus is a necessary tool for our existence; and finally, the inner being—call it heart or psyche or soul or all three—is the center of who we are and the emotional structure on which we stand.

People feel a great many things and imagine inexplicably more. Feelings and imagination are not tangible substances but defining aspects of the stuff driving the heart's workings. These two are like the wind; without an iota of physical substance we can see, what is felt or imagined enables or hinders decision-making and thus our behavior. The question all people will eventually ask is whether feelings or imagination matter, and if so, to what degree?

Consider just one instance of the heart shaping our decisions: the feeling of insecurity, those moments of feeling awkward or vulnerable. Individual reactions to insecurity result in decisions to move forward or retreat. Developing patterns of advancing or retreating behavior, spurred by feelings of insecurity, is learned behavior. One person may know a determined pattern based on "I will," despite the insecurity, while another person retreats behind the words, "I can't." The dichotomy between these two types of individuals gives rise to the labels of *agent* and *victim*.

The pervasive cultural value of self-hood assumes the stronger position of agent-status is built and maintained by believing in one's self. Self-developed confidence sounds like the best way to be human. The widely accepted belief in oneself promotes self-reliance as the path of confidence and fulfillment. However, individual reliance must logically reject anything outside itself as better, and that means the rejection of God. Reliance on self frequently pushes the individual toward agnosticism or atheism.

Emotional growth as a person flourishes when inner security is discovered and maintained. The cultural maxim to "Believe in yourself," stands on this reality of truth. Inner security broadens the development of self-awareness and produces keen insight into motives that can reshape our goals. Understanding ourselves strengthens us for achievement. Security within allows processing of life's circumstances in the best possible way. As an individual, you may develop yourself emotionally into something better. This is the expectation of maturation generally. The problem is the self isn't

I is for Illumination

completely trustworthy! It's the sin nature problem, our selfishness. Believing in oneself is not only limiting, it will always stand against God's will.

The emotional forces with which we all wrestle include others' expectations and feelings. Intellectual forces are frequently blind to eternal truths. Governing laws stir highly charged emotional issues, and the educational system directs elitist humanism as the guiding light of truth. Both group and institutional forces are outside of us. Within, we have our emotional reactions and needs.

Humans need intimacy with God to gain a sense of adequacy and develop as agents in this life. When an individual's purpose is drawn from the depths of the pure love of the Creator, there is an unparalleled sense of being.

Lift your vision! The authentic self you were intended to be is a function of the Presence of the Holy Spirit in your heart, guiding and comforting. Also, remember that in the Word, we are exhorted to grow into the maturity of Jesus (Eph 4:11–13).[5] There is no greater security, and therefore, no greater peace than that which is known by trusting in God. Our need for intimacy with our Creator is profound. Intimacy with him stabilizes the heart, instructs the intellect, sustains a working conscience, and guides choices of interactions with others and society in general.

To live without God is like driving a car in the dark on a rural road: no headlights, no streetlights, and no lights from other vehicles. It's a wild, insecure, moving gamble to keep the car on the road and arrive anywhere safely. Believing in one's self as a safe driver is not enough.

Life in the spirit of the Lord Jesus is more than just an enlightenment of values. It is the illumination of absolute truth. As humans, we cannot fathom the fullness of all things as God does. Yet, because the Son, Jesus, walked among us and taught about the Father, we can become bearers of the same light of truth. In oneness with God, the state of intimacy with him, our emotional and intellectual "sight" is illuminated by his absolute truth. It gets better!

God's plan for each person who comes into his Spirit is to learn a growing depth of awareness of his wisdom. This in-the-spirit individual will experience guidance and comfort that resolves the confusing moral dilemmas raised by individuals, the culture, and governing authority. Spiritual/emotional insight is directly consequential from intimacy with

---

5. Paraphrases adapted from the New American Standard Bible: ©2020 by the Lockman Foundation.

the indwelling Holy Spirit. Love of self becomes understood in the secure freedom to love others. The will of one's emotional framework is ordered and empowered, giving the deepest sense of self through the relationship with God.

Walking with the Lord Jesus, known within our being by his Spirit, illuminates the eyes of the heart with his love and wisdom. The life our God intends for his creation becomes a day-to-day intimacy with the Holy Spirit—seek him and experience it. Everyone who is born again is given the Holy Spirit (Eph 1:13; Tim 3:5). Turn on the light of truth in your heart. This is not a poetic metaphor. Christians may be heard lamenting, "I'm in a spiritual desert," or "I'm in a dry time." Intimacy with Father God is the opposite.

He offers the fullness of himself from the moment spirit-life begins, and he remains supremely faithful. Dry times simply mean that we have unwittingly put down the cup of living water. Take responsibility and return to trusting in him, regardless of the circumstances. The born-again believer is a child of God with the prerogative to seek him. Yet, it is the believer's initiative to reach for Father God's offered hand, which results in deepening intimacy (Rev 3:20). We choose the frequency of contact over the long haul of life, the opening and moving in trust, any offering in warmth of our supplications, or just speaking to him all our thoughts. In other words, like any true friend in a platonic relationship, God is fully invested in intimacy from his side of the relationship. The depth of experiencing that intimacy rides on the level of investment the believer places in the relationship. The heart longing to know intimacy with God exercises an embrace in the mind and from the heart to accept the love and holiness of God. We willingly take upon ourselves the yoke of humility, gentleness, and love (Matt 11:25–30).

The process of learning spirit-life is marked by a growing facility to measure interactions in the material world with what the Bible references as spiritual eyes and ears, a frequent idiom spoken by Jesus (Mark 4:23; Luke 14:35; Matt 13:16; Mark 8:18). On a personal level, intimacy with God supports the maturing-in-spirit experience by building sensitivity to and understanding of his personal affirmations and encouragements. Assurance of his personal watch-care is truly living water in the desert! Intimacy with the Father God through the indwelling Holy Spirit is the source of illumination from Jesus' life, establishing all order and strength in the believer.

J is for Jesus, the Judge
Justification, Judgment, Justice

For thirty-four years, I taught children across grades four through eight. A vital teaching skill was classroom management. If I did not keep twenty to twenty-five children focused and engaged in planned activities, that resulted in acquired knowledge and understanding, I failed. Without a well-managed classroom, I could not accomplish the prime directive—cause student learning.

Management meant gaining meaningful compliance from those in my charge. As you may have noticed in school, kids will sometimes deliberately try to get around rules and expectations. Maybe you have tried to get out of the work that helps build understanding, as well. We humans often resist what is in our best interests, but that is another topic.

Whenever I spotted a student directly undermining the progress of other students' learning or being self-distracted, professionalism required I address the situation. I had to restore orderly progress for all. Ironically, I could exert authority poorly and create more disruption. Successful management occurred when I intervened as little as possible. Sometimes eye contact followed by a raised eyebrow from me sufficed to redirect a student's behavior. In the case of behavior disrupting others, I would extend to the student a low-key invitation for a visit at my desk, where we engaged in quiet conversation.

"Susie, you were not on task with the reading and response prompt written on the board."

"I was just writing a note. It wasn't going to take too much time."

Clearly, Susie didn't see a problem with her lack of engagement. In fact, her use of the word *just* illustrates plainly how she viewed the entire moment. Her choice to be off task was, in her mind, not anything concerning.

She justified her lack of engagement in the classroom by diminishing the significance of her non-compliance. This student's reaction to me and the use of *just* was repeated a hundred times every school year and is typical human behavior. I frequently hear adults do the same.

Humans consistently want the freedom to exercise personal choice as individuals. However, those choices often prioritize irresponsible behavior based on justification and are frequently just an excuse. Texting while driving is a great example of shirking one's own safety and the safety of others explained as, "I was just thumbing a few little letters." Does the act of texting justify the physical harm or property damage caused by the distracted driver? Total a car as I have while driving, and this lesson is painfully clear. We all think at some time or another that our chosen poor judgment is acceptable. We all are capable of thinking highly of all our decisions and thereby entering the land of the unwise (Rom 12:3).[1]

Middle school students are learning to think for themselves. As a teacher, I understood I was hearing my students express age-appropriate immaturity and the influence of the parents at home. Students reflect their home's atmosphere and rhetoric. There are wildly varied opinions and dispositions found across the United States regarding what personal freedom encompasses. Clearly, U.S. citizens share the value of individual freedom.

Think about the duality of *freedom*: those granted by law and those freedoms known emotionally. The first is about the legal structure governing one's physical actions, particularly when the well-being of others may be impacted. The second is being free from the expectations or manipulations of other people.

The laws that rule over us may or may not seem just. Nonetheless, we are responsible for living by them. Most citizens respond to written law with compliance or mostly compliant decisions. A few people will be fastidious complying to all laws. Most people will engage in violating minor offenses if they believe there are no consequences. Driving above the posted speed limit is a good example. A relatively small number of people live in deliberate lawlessness. General attitudes toward obedience to written laws are all over the map within U.S. culture; and I expect the same is found in other countries.

We also confront limits on personal freedoms as exercised by people holding authority over us: employers and classroom teachers for examples. In unstructured relational situations, what other people think of us and how

---

1. Paraphrases adapted from the New American Standard Bible: ©2020 by the Lockman Foundation.

J is for Jesus, the Judge

we are consequently treated is an emotional weight. We may feel ourselves burdened, entrapped, or manipulated. Navigating the exercise of personal freedom requires successful compliance with legitimate authority, and wise responsiveness to the opinions and attitudes of all the people in one's life.

Thinking in these terms illustrates the concept and action of *judgment*. Consistent with our positive and negative reality, judgment is fair or unfair. The difference can even be a matter of judgment. We all experience being unfairly judged, and we have all engaged in unfairly judging others. It can be hurtful when the person who is being judgmental is important to us; and if we are the ones being judgmental, then we cause harm.

Judging others occurs within Christian churches. There are two sides to this: other Christians observing us and experiencing the impact of our choices fairly address our sinful behavior; and on the flip side of that situation, we are confronted with being unfairly judged by someone's self-righteousness. What is the difference between a friend challenging us to grow beyond an observed fault, and a self-righteous person subjecting us to their personal standards of morality? To ask the caring friend to stop being judgmental is the error of unwise self-protection. Emotional maturity develops as we sharpen our self-awareness through admitting our weaknesses and faults. To satisfy self-righteous judgments from others is submission to legalism, and that moves one's inner being in the opposite direction from life in the spirit of Christ.

Call self-righteousness hiding behind Christian labels *religionism* and the practicioner a *religionist*. There exists in these hearts an intense perception of right and wrong based on any given Christian dogma. A judgmental religionist feels required to correct others. In contrast, a fellow-believer using truthful, loving feedback for the development of our self-awareness is a God-ordained construct. The former is judgmentalism. The latter is fair evaluation of behavior.

In confrontations of any kind about personal behavior, our self-defensive response will be varied. Examples include:

- The duck method, "I think I will avoid this person from now on; they're too toxic."
- The antagonistic, judgmental rejoinder, "I see this and this wrong in *your* life!"
- Self-righteous indignation, "How dare you say such a thing to me!"

- A few will question as if to understand by saying, "What leads you to conclude that about me." However, responsible change does not manifest.

In these scenarios exists an underlying aversion to self-examination of personal behavior. That aversion ascends to the fore as a function of pride.

A sincere desire to be in the spirit listens to what is being said with an openness for self examination. There are three responses that facilitate a beneficial outcome:

- withdraw for consideration of the feedback then follow-up later; or
- agree, ask for forgiveness, and seek growth to greater maturity; or
- with sincere thanks for the speaker's concern, reply with disagreement.

In the third option above, there is a need for maintaining good will through humility. What always governs our interactions with other believers and particularly so in the situation of building spiritual maturity in one another is Ephesians 4:1-3: the unity of the Spirit in the bond of peace.

In choosing any one of these responses, we seek the fullness of God's will. The willingness to engage with a loving friend over one's behavior is the soil that growth in spirit maturation requires. When such confrontations occur, there will likely be a moment of resentment in one's heart. That is old nature emotions. Maturity recognizes that pride stirs up resentment, ignores this inner negative prod, and responds instead with respect.

What if you feel the confrontation is based on self-righteousness? The fix is a bit counter-intuitive. "Do not judge, so that you will not be judged. For in the way you judge, you will be judged; and by your standard of measure, it will be measured to you," found in Matthew 7:1-2. These are clear words we read from Jesus. The Lord Jesus instructs all believers here not to qualify as evil the motives, the inner heart, of anothers' words or actions. We cannot be certain we know either the motivations or the maturity level of the one speaking to us. The confrontation calls us to evaluate only what to do in response. Wisdom focuses on what is openly spoken to us.

In choosing not to judge, we find freedom for our soul. Obedience to the command not to judge is a source of gaining spirit insight. We learn to forbear, to forgive, or to govern our own speech with grace. "Blessed are the pure in heart, for they shall see God," is a promise found in Matthew 5:8. Putting away judgmental attitudes clears the heart to see more clearly the Presence of God and gauge the moving of the Spirit of God.

J is for Jesus, the Judge

When on the other side of this situation, and the behavior of another believer appears sinful remember this ironic twist: whatever you say judgmentally about others is possibly a judgment that could be said against yourself. Psychology identifies a behavioral phenomenon called *projection*. This is hard to recognize and occurs when unresolved self-importance, self-hatred, or selfish desire blinds us to our own faults; yet, we see that fault in other people.[2] In light of this, Matthew 7:1–2 above becomes more relevant and powerful.

The spirit-life allows us to let down our guard and false attempts at building our own self-esteem. Developing an attitude of not judging and turning the other cheek emotionally when confronted by hard or hurtful judgmental attitudes is a deepening of our experience of the Spirit of the Lord. Spirit-life self control holds the believer in openness to love in all situations and establishes one's sense of comfort in the Holy Spirit, a protection from the self-righteous judgments of others.

The needed way forward in mutual interactions with other believers is the receiving of Christ's instruction and admonition. Humbling ourselves in obedience to his ways, the heart finds the freedom to love others and forbear much. This is spiritual power. It rides on surpassing confidence in God's goodness and his promise to right wrongs against us (Rom 12:17–19). There is justice in the kingdom of God which is administered by the Lord. Whether the fullness of that justice is worked out in this life or is settled finally at the Great White Throne Judgment, we can be confident that all injustice will be righted (Rev 20:11).

---

2. "Projection." *Psychology Today*.

K is for Kingdom Kin
Kill, Kindness, Kindred

THE CONSTANT MEDIA NEWS of humans killing humans is a hard, drumming noise. The boyfriend kills the girlfriend; the terrorist explodes a bomb in the market; a troubled youth opens fire randomly in a school; one gang attacks another; countries use force against one another killing soldiers and civilians. We hear the news anchor relate the bloodshed and experience the story as horrible, insane, or inhumane. Such news feeds fear.

We rarely fear that we might become a killer. Humans are all potential killers, though. That is, from God's perspective. Jesus clearly warns that being angry with someone carries guilt equal to murder (Matt 5:21–22).[1] But, we humans keenly draw lines of degree. Murder is wrong, but we rationalize that anger toward someone is unavoidable. It is not hard to grasp that a link exists between hatred, vitriol, and murder.

Look over social media and recognize how quickly users attack what others do or say with judgment-based insults. The angry noise of put-downs and more disturbing threats flows unmitigated. Explore the Scriptures about hatred of others; how we "murder" with our words is settled with clarity.

People who do not know our Lord spot and condemn hateful speech. The voices are many and loud who insist accepting others is a fundamental proposition of a just society. These voices shout, sing, and posit how the United States must embrace positive change. The demands for fair treatment of all people is ubiquitous with a small exception: anyone with an opposing political view. What is ugly and therefore intolerable, and what is reasonable and tolerable language? Many claiming Christ will insult those

---

1. Paraphrases adapted from the New American Standard Bible: ©2020 by the Lockman Foundation.

with liberal political views, and conversely, liberals proclaim tolerance for everyone but will bash Christians with angry insults.

Here's an example from this week's headlines: an assistant professor employed by Old Dominion University in Norfolk, Virginia, resigned over a language issue.[2] What usage landed the assistant professor in the middle of an uproar? The scholar developed a term for research reporting, which intended to label people who experience sexual attraction toward children without sounding negative. The phrase used which damaged the instructor's reputation was "minor-attracted person" (MAP).[3] It resembles the phrase "same-sex attracted person" used as a label for many members of the LGBTQ community. (Some Christians acknowledge experiencing same-sex attraction but consider it sin to be overcome. They do not consider themselves as an LGBTQ person.) The scholar insisted the chosen descriptive tag was intended for people not actively practicing pedophilia but experiencing sexual attraction to minors. Nonetheless, the open revulsion of people to people manifesting this mental condition resulted in backlash against the university. The assistant professor resigned.

The fate of the assistant professor illustrates some behaviors, case in point pedophilia, are considered wrong by most everyone except those who practice the deluded desire. Beyond pedophilia, many issues have massive social approval but are stated as immoral in the Bible. Christians are labeled "haters" for agreeing with the moral expectations of the New Testament. This hate-labeling is part of the cost of believing the gospel of Jesus Christ (Matt 5:10).[4] We choose to be kind toward all people, but we must be faithful to the revelation of truth the Bible.

Kindness is a popular watchword these days as the solution to divisiveness in society. Kindness is an important principle, no doubt about that. However, as much as our culture needs acts of kindness and not acts of hatred, humans accept double standards and decry hatred except for selected, disliked individuals or groups.

People generally embrace an ambiguous framework for moral decisions. Across the current U.S. cultural landscape, an idealized view of accepting all people intends a moral proposition in support of the deep human need for connection with others. That acceptance, however, is not

---

2. Flaherty, "Scholar Resigns."

3. Flaherty, "Scholar Resigns."

4. Paraphrases adapted from the New American Standard Bible: ©2020 by the Lockman Foundation.

upheld for people holding moral or political positions against one's own ideals. The ambiguous moral dilemma at the root of our cultural angst is antithetical ideals. On one side is a principle that human connection is valuable and needed; we all belong to humanity. On the other side is a rationalized practice of rejecting, even seeking the punishment of, those who espouse contrary ideals. We are arguing over who belongs to the participatory political union and who does not. The sense and experience of commonality as one humanity lies crushed in the conflict of ideals.

Our need for human connection crosses the boundaries of the political divide. What we as a linked political entity cannot find are the cohesive relational capabilities rooted in a *kinship* experience. In healthy families, a sense of unconditional belonging develops intentionally for each member. Kinship as an emotional construct may include people who are not of the same bloodline. An identifiable cultural trend is to define family not as those of a shared bloodline, but as friends who have forged a strong sense of belonging to one another. Family as a concept is now frequently regarded as the chosen few one knows and accepts unconditionally.

All humans search for and need a sense of belonging within a group. (Recall the discussion of attachment as a basic psychological need.) In our culture, it is common for young people who share and enjoy the same entertainments will naturally hang out and become friends. If two or three, or four people like the same music, food, and activities, then friendship is likely to follow. That is, as long as one meets the conditional framework of the group and acts in solidarity within the limits dictated by some common denominator. Liking the same objects as a means for establishing a friendship is a naive idea and usually discovered to be a fallacy by the late teen years.

A relationship begun by identifying mutually common likes within the material world is unlikely to last a lifetime if for no other reason than people's tastes will change over time. The natural place, though, where such relationships break is that a shallow reason to be together doesn't feed our emotional needs. These deeper emotional states are where we desire honest connection with one another. A more satisfying sense of kinship is with those who share similar outlooks on life based on shared values. Friendships stemming from these essential themes in life frequently develop a strong sense of belonging.

Groups we frequently enter in life may contain language suggestive of the deep connections of kinship. Work associations in which the professional atmosphere is friendly and supportive may foster statements like, "We are family around here." However, a collegial work atmosphere is not kinship. The desire for professional growth will lead workers to exit relationships for a new job. Gangs are a severe and harmful environment where the group's expectations demand compliance as the price of being a member. The demanded loyalty to the gang is framed within a false identification as belonging to a family.

Religion describes the parameters of a shared experience, as well. A deep sense of kinship or relatedness because of the standard dogma of belief may result. Yet, failure to meet group expectations may carry blatant messages of disapproval. The disapproval may be a direct rebuke for serious violations of group expectations or subtle, unexplained censure for apparent non-conformity. The nonconforming member may maintain official membership while kinship with fellow members weakens. The nature and depth-level of a sense of belonging that develops from group associations varies like all human-to-human interpersonal relations.

The topic of belonging to groups, from ad hoc cliques to purposely organized and continuing institutions, raises hard questions. How and where does anyone find a deep, satisfying sense of connection, of belonging, which earns the "kinship" label? Are the strongest rewards a function of conditional group acceptance? Is the price of conformity to others' expectations too high a price for gaining a sense of belonging? Does any group offer unconditional love?

Life in the spirit of God brings the most profound sense of being "kindred spirits." When two or more people share an understanding of the Presence of Jesus within them, their depth of kinship grows unmatched by associations of any other human commonality. Inside a circle of people knowing Christ together a profound opportunity will unfold. The experience of being forgiven and the resulting emotional state flowing from being loved unconditionally creates a desire to unconditionally love others. A desire grows to learn the depths of the love of God. An emotional equipping for the highest level of love is discovered in the spirit. The spirit function of his available Holy Spirit feeding our spirit shapes all relationships through active application of the love described in 1 Corinthians 13.

Beyond the family of believers, we encounter open society with the same love in the heart. Though that society is not equipped to trust us. We prove the will and glory of God as we exhibit and offer sacrificial love to those around us. No act of kindness is a futile effort. Yet, random acts of kindness are not enough to overcome evil with good. Being in the spirit equips a believer with kindness in every situation.

In-the-spirit kindness is more than a religious affirmation that kindness exists "out there, somewhere," and one should try it sometime. Mature spirit life acts true to Romans 12 instruction, we offer peace with all and love our enemies; and consistent with 1 Corinthians 5:12–13 instruction, we do not judge those outside the church.

In the spirit, we enter kinship with other Christians. With those outside of the kingdom of God, we express respect and concern for their well-being from our hearts. Thus, in the Holy Spirit, we are equipped to interact with those both within and outside the kingdom. A shared adoration of Jesus continually deepens kinship with other believers across decades. Sharing God's kindness with all those around you satisfies the soul.

L is for the Life in Jesus's Spirit
Libertine, Legalist, Light

THE LIBERTINE IS THE human who looks at life and carves out his or her individual experience of sexuality in tandem with personal freedom. Also in the definition is the nuance that such a thinker thinks freely, separated from any restrictions of religion.[1] The discourse herein expends many words on the sins of the human race, however, in today's world, pain spirals outward from sexual immorality. We examine sexuality not through specific behaviors but with a spiritual lens on the inherent motivations.

The body is physically mature and ready for procreation at the end of puberty. Humans are not typically considered instinct-driven animals. Nonetheless, the hormones that drive sexual interest are natural, powerful, and can override logical reasoning. The sexual drive feels instinctual. If perceived as uncontrollable, it leads to sexual activity. Indeterminate sexual activity results in practical problems for the individuals engaging in it. An unwanted pregnancy is a tragedy for the new life conceived, and a difficult, often painful situation for both parents. Even more so for young parents.

Looking around, it is not hard to tell from media—film, social, and print—that physical intimacy is a mainstay of many individual lifestyles. A common belief and expectation in our culture is that people will have multiple physically intimate relationships throughout their lifetime. In line with this frequency, the world spirit describes and expects physical intimacy will be explored as a teen transitions into adulthood. Much of contemporary culture celebrates sexual freedom as a right of adults and offers teens the guidance to indulge in sexuality responsibly—meaning avoid activity that produces a child.

---

1. Merriam-Webster, *libertine*, 670.

According to Scripture, the Lord has a different intent for humanity. Jesus states physical intimacy is intended for one monogamous, lifelong relationship (Matt 19:6).[2] A significant divide exists between living in the spirit of Jesus and living in the world's chaotic system. Jesus is clear on this matter. A union of one man and one woman in marriage is the only God-authorized and blessed circumstance for the physical one-flesh experience (Mark 10:6–9). Therefore, Christianity since its beginnings has stipulated abstinence from sexual relationships outside of marriage. The key to managing this mandate rests fully in seeking maturity of the new spirit-being.

Finding one's destiny in the ways of the Lord stems from finding maturity in spirit. The active pursuit of that maturity becomes a personal responsibility at the moment of being born of the spirit. For teens reared in Christian homes, an early experience of commitment to Christ is common. Approaching adulthood as a Christian teen is often a fork in the road: accept responsibility for personal behavior and embrace Christian spirituality; or choose a path ungoverned by the Spirit of Jesus.

Consequently, for the teenager reaffirming commitment to Christ as the inner state on which one enters adulthood, the admonition for maintaining self-control is accepted. The practice of abstaining from sexual intimacy until marriage is a test, a crucible for some. Abstinence becomes definitive of what it means to know one's identity as the new creature in the spirit. The authentic Christian experience is far more than commitment to rule-keeping in the name of Christianity. Authentic spirit life develops an understanding of sexual purity as a result of living in and through the Holy Spirit. The contrasting and incorrect perception of abstinence is that of a goodness goal that is checked off as accomplished or not.

Unfortunately, there exists a group of people found across denominational lines who practice an adherence to right rules as insurance of satisfying God's expectations. Such belief systems justify themselves with Scripture, though frequently the hearts of the adherents are hard or troubled. The result is legalism, an approach to Christianity claiming fidelity to Scripture.

A legalist upholds a relationship with God that reflects the Mosaic Covenant given in the Old Testament. The Mosaic Covenant delivered the Ten Commandments, and clearly stated the relationship with God as a conditional interaction. Following this framework, the legalist will speak

---

2. Paraphrases adapted from the New American Standard Bible: ©2020 by the Lockman Foundation.

L is for the Life in Jesus's Spirit

foremost about obedience to the commands given in both Old and New Testaments. Though mention will be made of the Holy Spirit, legalistic perspectives expect conformity of behavior but offer little instruction on the development of union with the Holy Spirit. As a general label, a rule-based emphasis for Christian living is called *legalism*.

Jesus is recorded in John 6:63, saying, "It is the Spirit who gives life; the flesh profits nothing; the words that I have spoken to you are spirit and are life." Paul states in 2 Cor 3:5–6, "Not that we are adequate in ourselves to consider anything as coming from ourselves, but our adequacy is from God, who also made us adequate as servants of a new covenant, not of the letter but of the Spirit; for the letter kills, but the Spirit gives life." Jesus declares, and Paul describes that rule-keeping intended to prove our adequacy as Christians does not afford us the life of God in the spirit. An authentic Christian life is the life in the spirit; the heartbeat of the spirit life is the supernatural indwelling of God within a believer.

Spirit-life is enjoying a loving relationship with God. Love for God desires obedience to the will of God. All determined actions of disobedience spring from loving oneself more than God. Rather than attempting to make the old nature do the imperatives and abstain from the prohibitions, the regenerated human receives the light of truth and godly love from Jesus. Living means being immersed in a process of growth as the new spirit from him and continuing in him. Obedience is not merely an intellectual exercise of knowing rules. The born-again believer chooses the experience of emotional growth by practicing loving, godly interactions with others.

God is freedom from sin, and among other wonders, this understanding is a construct known as a result of experiencing the love from God. In its total sense, the spirit-life is a state of submission to the will of God. Spirit-life is an unparalleled satisfaction and a sense of meaning and purpose as a human. The phrase "the light of truth" is not poetic. It is a factual rendition of what it means to have our intellectual understanding tied to the commands of God.

A heart opened to the light of the Lord Jesus reorders both will and desire. Intellectual and emotional function are always a choice, and the light leads a believer into continual choosing of being in the spirit. In the authenticity of that simple phrase, we escape the pain resulting from libertine rejection of morality and find freedom from the legalism of rule-sequenced behavior. Jesus is the life of God and the light of God, and he is our life in the spirit.

M is for the Meaning of Real
Milieu, Maximize, Metaphysics

Dear beloved reader, you are living in a mess. That mess is the milieu of beliefs and power structures in your communities, nation, and around the globe. The world's religions, secular philosophies, current governments, the entertainment media, the corporations seeking to profit from you, and the teachers paid to educate you send messages intent on shaping and persuading you about the best way to live. There is significant disagreement among the sources.

Added to the confusion of these diverse and influential voices are multiple complications exerting pressure on the experience of living. A few to name include the political strife within government, climate change, the forces of a global economy, crime, and competition for jobs. Stir into that turbulent mix the ingredient that anyone with whom you interact on a daily basis is prone to emotional reactions in any given moment. The finished stew tastes of massive anxiety. Yikes!! *How* will you determine your path through all of this? There are two practical means to that end.

Passing through the late teen years in a Christian home, trust your parents and honor their rules and guidance.[1] The wisdom of God determined the family as the place where the young would best be developed in preparation for adult life. Yes, parents do not know everything, nor is all they say or do perfect. Certainly none of the entities identified in the first paragraph above love you even a little. Well, maybe some of the teachers at

---

1. This book is written assuming the reader is a youth in a Christian home. It is certainly possible such is not the case, and therefore some phrasing herein may be inapplicable. The author was reared by non-Christian parents, who were both given to alcohol excess. God is able to meet any reader in the exact circumstances being experienced.

school have loved their students, but that love was only for a season, not for the whole of anyone's life.

Secondly, and the point of this book, as an older teen weighing varied paths and options know what is real about God, and follow him. The goal here is a framework intended to help the reader grasp the enormity of God, the beauty of his holiness, the depths of his love, and the efficacy of life lived in his Spirit.

Remember, neither the sun nor storms, but the rudder gives a boat direction; neither reward nor pain determines a life course. Life as a human is not defined by the circumstances faced but by the decisions made in response to the circumstances. Naysayers will counter my assertion here with an unequivocal, "That's not true! Economic factors, intelligence level, and societal opportunity beyond personal control all influence one's destiny." The naysayers are describing the box, not the person inside it.

The challenge is to adequately assess the material world, the box. The world system can be difficult to navigate, especially from a monetary perspective. However, life has never been consistently fair in distributing equal opportunity. Humans face an observable variation of factors. For example, my dad was an alcoholic, which substantially impacted our family. While many other dads among my classmates may have been alcoholics, the families with non-alcoholic dads were more numerous. This one factor alone divides any class of students into unequal realities.

As a person matures, opportunities and obstacles related to the nurturing received during the formative years will be encountered. Ultimately, each individual has personal power over choice in confronting outside circumstances. The responsibility of an adult is to prioritize responding to life's circumstances whether these be opportunities or obstacles.

As a result of this dilemma—destiny as personal responsibility but an unequal playing field—much anger rises across the U.S. population. However, even if the field were made equal for everyone, those who embrace personal responsibility and engage in conscientious work will gain the most influence over personal destiny.

The takeaway point is that there is a commonality of motivational strategy across today's education, sports, the arts, and other human endeavors. That commonality is the only real power an individual possesses is the ability to change themselves. Non-Christians and Christians alike hold to this maxim. The most critical factor affecting one's destiny, beloved, is personal decision-making. Will you choose what is good, authentic, and beautiful, or will you grasp for more stuff and notoriety? Experience and desire lead humans to want new states of being, that is, change. What does it mean to seek change that is not part of the Father's good will? To seek what is not from God will result in what does not satisfy the soul.

You may recognize a false message running around in the milieu of human experience. Good experiences are sought, and extremely good experiences are the best! Good being a specifically subjective term. As a result, we are urged by the culture to always look for a better experience, the upgrade, super-size the meal or even better, make it all-you-can-eat; go first class; get all the options; bundle it; extend the warranty; play the lottery; go big or go home; and on and on—get the maximum out of life.

Books, movies, and plays frequently depict one or more characters as greedy. Dial back the greed, and a slightly different human experience surfaces in many characters, an unrelenting desire for a satisfying life. Looking for satisfaction is as simple as adding a little salt to the stew, as complicated as investing in the stock market, or as logical as seeking a pay raise—again. We, humans, share an intrinsic desire for satisfaction, and we want it for our bodies, minds, and emotions.

The reason for writing about seeking satisfaction—no doubt, you have felt this drive—is because many souls seeking satisfaction have gone down some very unhealthy paths. In other words, just because a desire exists does not thereby equal finding satisfaction. How can a young person tell? First, there is an important, complex word to grasp. This word may not be common in everyday conversations, but the concept is essential for a fulfilling life. That word is *metaphysics*, a major concept explored by poets, philosophers, and everyday better-path seekers. Contemplating the human experience often leads to the major topics of reality, truth, and beauty. Metaphysics examines the nature of reality and existence.[2]

What is considered real may seem straightforward enough. If something is tangible and visible, it is deemed real. Beyond just sight, the physical world known through all senses and in which our bodies exist is not that hard to understand as real. Yet, this material world has parts unseen by the naked eye. Examples are the molecular structure of stuff or even smaller, the atomic level. Also unseen is the inner being, though not composed of molecules, it is nonetheless real.

Shift from the physical world and consider the intangible aspects of thoughts, feelings, and imagination; it leads to the discussion of spirituality.

---

2. Merriam Webster's, *metaphysics*, 731.

M is for the Meaning of Real

The journey through the outer physical world is navigated by engaging the inner, intangible reality. The best possible direction in life results from the impact of desire becoming applied thinking. Therefore, the direction or course of our material existence improves as the immaterial inner life of emotions, imagination, and thinking becomes ordered and purposeful.

Many self-help books, whether encouraging Eastern mysticism or offering secular psychological therapies, provide guidance on achieving this inner order. However, none compare to the spiritual life found in the Holy Spirit of Jesus Christ. Western religious tradition mentions the Holy Spirit, but practical teaching on ordering the inner reality lacks a consensus of how Christians enter, develop, and practice the connection to the Holy Spirit. That lack of consensus creates disunity between Christian groups and confusion among individuals.

The highest, truest, most real human experience is finding and being in God's Spirit. The walk in the spirit is a wonder! The depths of the Lord God —Father, Son, and Holy Spirit—open as the believer seeks the inner path through life according to the revelation of the Scripture. Jesus is recorded in Matthew 7:7-11 saying, "Seek, and you will find; knock, and it shall be opened to you; ask, and it will be given." I am confident that here is the best advice needed for life: trust the Bible as the revealed truth of the human experience; and seek the revelation of the Lord. You will discover the way of the spirit. In the spirit, self-discipline over bodily desires will manifest; the mind will see and develop in line with truth; the heart—all of your emotions—will order through God's love; and the "real" of you is established. One of life's profound and challenging questions is answered.

God is real and the only possible Source of anyone knowing what is real. To help you trust the God of the Bible, I highly recommend you read *I Don't Have Enough Faith to be an Atheist* by Norm Geisler and Frank Turek.

N is for Nascent Strength
Neurotic, Negativity, Necessary

WE LIVE IN AN extreme age beyond people wanting over-the-top experiences. Extreme states of emotional distress can drive common negative behaviors. Exhibiting a pattern of negative behaviors was once labeled a neurosis and was considered the beginning of mental illness.[1] However, what was considered neurotic is now labeled a personality disorder.[2] These disorders are linked to anxiety, depression, and inner conflicts.[3] Anyone having a rough day might behave poorly as a result. The issue that marks a possible personality disorder is a negative pattern disrupting an individual's overall responsible functioning.

It is likely you have experienced or observed someone else acting negatively under pressure. Behaviors like being irritated, emotional distress over everyday events, inability to get along with others, or over-reaction to neutral events may be the result of bad day. However, if these types of behaviors are a regular pattern, the person may have developed a personality disorder. It brings to mind Jesus's words recorded in John 8:24, "Truly, truly, I say to you, everyone who commits sin is the slave of sin."

In my own experience, high levels of anxiety have sparked emotionally charged reactions such as antagonistic sarcasm, flaring temper, resentfulness, or attempting manipulation of others. I have observed the same in people generally. Behaviors stemming from anxiety may become ingrained as habitual action or inaction. Emotional immaturity will often use negative behavior as a coping mechanisms. Coping, however, may take the turn of avoiding a difficult truth. When a learned coping mechanism

1. Key, "Neurotic Behavior," WebMD.
2. Key, "Neurotic Behavior," WebMD.
3. Key, "Neurotic Behavior," WebMD.

N is for Nascent Strength

becomes an identified facet of a person's behavior, it might be described as a personality trait. It might also be a "personality disorder." An unchanging emotional state that controls behaviors can feel restrictive like a chain. Feedback from others or other life consequence, may help an individual identify the anxiety condition.

I write this as a warning that anyone may develop and be controlled by emotionally-based, negative habit patterns. As a matter of self-care, it is vital to recognize that unresolved fears are a fundamental cause of personal anxiety; and anxiety stunts spiritual well-being and growth. Occasional outbursts of negative behavior is part of growing up. Be honest with yourself and do not blame personal poor reactions on outside factors. Yes, something outside of you triggered your reaction. Gaining control of your inward being and managing responses, however, is a personal responsibility.

Personal growth in our emotional life stems from gaining self-awareness of our deep motivations. One of our deepest motivators is the avoidance of what we fear. Fear is a natural inner state and inclines one toward avoidance of emotional growth. Life has ways, though, that force confrontations over negative behavior. The consequences for habitual negative behavior are often painful. That pain may drive any person deeper into avoidance. However, it also confronts the individual with a nagging need for emotional growth. Upon gaining self-awareness later in life about my own issues with procrastination, I discovered that my unwillingness to start most things was a coping strategy to avoid a fear of performing poorly.

How can anybody gain needed self-awareness and avoid developing locked-in negative behavior? How *might* the average person become self-aware of needed emotional growth? No one dedicates themselves to maturing in a skill, including emotional skill mastery, without first understanding their starting level. Accurate self-evaluation is the starting point, followed by taking personal responsibility for growth.

The person seeking emotional development has a ready resource: pay attention to one's thoughts and spoken words. Look for mental or verbal expressions of frustration, anger, or anxiety. Such negative thoughts or speech may indicate that present stress factors stimulate a fear of some sort. A good example is one's anxious statements responsively erupting under pressure, like complaints as discussed previously. Our emotional states of frustration, anger, or anxiety reveal something unsettled within our inner being. The unsettled inner reality may lead to verbal disparagement of others, lower self expectations, identifying worse case scenarios, and general, negative cliches of personal failings. The evidence of the inner conflict is false or exaggerated statements about others or ourselves. Such negative words are like a malfunction warning light on a digital display.

Unreasonable fears or assumptions about oneself create a negative undertow on our perceptions of what is desired and expected from life. The negativity fruits from anxiety and related but unrelieved fear. Practical biblical instruction regarding actual negative circumstances exists, and this instruction can be learned for confronting negative self-assessment: "Rejoice always." (1 Thes 5:16). Sounds impossible, but remember, all things are possible with God (Mark 10:27).[4] Purposeful refusal to express fearful or anxiety-laden words will stifle negative thoughts in the mind.

I am not encouraging to stuff one's feelings and pretend there is no problem. This is a replacement strategy: the negative thoughts and actions help to get our attention, but we can choose not to live in the negative. We choose to not engage in nor adopt negative thoughts or actions. We use the negative feelings to drive a search for understanding. We replace the natural human bent toward negative responses and seek an open heart that embraces gratitude and confident trust in God regardless of the circumstances. Rejoicing flows when anxiety or frustration is released, and genuine self-expression of trust is chosen. This strategy for self-management is an engagement of our new being laying hold of the light, love, and truth in the Holy Spirit.

The willingness to live in the old nature's fears and frustrations manifest from obstacles blocking our path toward goals. Remember our natural human need to seek self-enhancement? If we seek success only because family and friends expect it from us, we emotionally invest skill and talent as the path to gain approval for our performance. A lapse in performance, even momentarily, tempts us to complain over or blame-shift for the circumstances that opposed our success.

Religion and psychiatry both seek to help people reduce stress. Both note the effect of positive thinking as a tool against fears and anxieties. Being positive is a definite plus! If stopping negativity is the goal, positive thinking and related expressions are valuable tools. Negatives, whether a gripe, grumble, lament, moan, or defeatism will bias one's thinking and cause a focus on lists of obstacles, weaknesses, and lack of skills or funds.

---

4. Paraphrases adapted from the New American Standard Bible: ©2020 by the Lockman Foundation.

Negative bias undermines anyone's effectiveness. A positive shift in bias is an essential tool for bettering thinking skills.

However, being positive is a coping mechanism; it is not a cure for the inherent self-protectiveness predisposing humans to fear and anxiety. An individual who recognizes complaining or other negative behaviors and decides to counter with a more positive statement or action will grow toward emotional maturity. The more practiced positivism becomes, the greater the strength of the mechanism, and there will be a connected reduction of anxiety and related fears. Yet, a positive mindset doesn't alter the root cause of anxiety-driven behavior.

Superior in every way to positive thinking is life in the Holy Spirit. Positivism is not needed. The eyes of the heart open in spirit-life. We see from a completely different vantage point when we are a new creature in Christ, literally born—created anew emotionally—as an image-bearer of God, which is his intent (Col 3:10).

Once you enter spirit-life by being born again, you have new abilities to live in the truth of love, joy, and peace. These nascent abilities will develop in response to regular exercise. The emotions grow and strengthen through exercise against resistance, just like muscles. For example, anxiety is the opposite of peace. The presence of anxiety is a marker of our old nature. If we process the release of the anxiety and replace it with peace as a state we inhabit by choice, we foster emotional growth. We remove the root of anxiety from which negative behaviors stem.

Choosing to trust in God is spiritual exercise with spiritual consequences. We resist natural human reactions and determine a supernatural path of developing and manifesting the fruit of the spirit. God meets us with what we seek. The Scriptures reveal the truth that our humanness without Christ is the fallen nature, and it is the driving life experience before regeneration begins. The individual who knows the Presence of the indwelling Christ learns to identify and reject the old nature and grows in the ability to live as a new creature born of the spirit (1 Cor 2:6–16). Negative, even harmful, emotional states root from selfish natural drives and result in overall reactions and poor decisions. Moving into spiritual peace from a place of material anxiety is a turn up the path of faith.

Jesus said that if you sin, you are a slave to sin. In first century Israel, there were no terms like *neurotic* or *personality disorder*. No doubt, people had negative emotions and related behaviors disrupting their personal lives and the lives of others. We can presume anxieties of being human in the 1st century were as compelling as they are now. Thus, the words of Jesus about being freed by the truth apply to finding release from emotional habits rooted in anxiety and fear (John 8:32).

Our modern understanding of mental-emotional health develops intellectually in words not available to first-century authors. However, we may still apply New Testament language to situations now labeled as conditions of emotional health. Anxiety is a fruit of the fallen nature. In the spirit of Christ is an emotional framework. Anxiety and related fear are not found in Christ. In God's spiritual economy, we may exchange our fallen nature's emotional bent for the emotional stature of life in Christ.

Beloved reader, know the Scripture, trust and follow the Scripture, meet the living Holy Spirit of Jesus, and choose to walk in the life only Jesus can supply (John 1:4–5). "Taking off" the old nature and "putting on" the new sound complicated or enigmatic. However, the willful act of changing our emotional focus is the path of freedom out of unmanageable negative forces within our first-born human nature. Seeking understanding of Truth known in Christ Jesus, then choosing the new life in him is basic and necessary for the experience of authentic Christianity.

O is for Open-ended Obedience
Opposition, Order, Overcoming

IN BOTH CHAMBERS OF a bicameral U.S. Congress, in corporation board rooms atop executive towers, across all state capitol legislative chambers, and within every other administrative board of leaders sharing oversight responsibilities, there exists a common tool. A tool most teens in high school classrooms will be taught and expected to use: debate. Debate serves the purpose of allowing varied points of view on any proposition to be openly compared based on significant facts. Often, speakers will use a context of idealized values in addition to just the facts. The open review of opposing positions informs and intends influence on voting members. When it works, we call the progress an achievement of order.

In the day to day world, opposing viewpoints and related individual choices are not structured debates. From casual group associations down to just two people relating, discussions like debate reveal support for or opposition against the opinions of others. This is a fact of life. Across varied social levels, differences of viewpoint and related opinion carry the potential to cause friction. Friction developing can devolve into arguments, and there are no real rules of order to be invoked and applied. The emotional friction experienced by opposing opinions are a stressful hazard of living within the society around us.

We will each know multiple levels of one to one relationships. Swift and non-binding is the brief exchange with service counter personnel. Classmate relationships, choirs, sports teams, and club memberships last for months or at most a few years, and significant family and some friends are expected life-long interactions. All levels of one to one interaction produce opposing opinions on topics large and small; discomforting is a resulting argument.

The more significant the role a person holds in one's life, the more consequential a difference of opinion becomes. At any level, unresolved differences of opinion or any related arguing produces stress on body and mind. Unaddressed by healing reconciliation, broken personal relationships may result in emotional maladjustment.

Recognize that on your side of these relationships, you face one of two challenges: a battleground of wills or a proving ground for emotional growth. It takes a bit of wisdom to bypass the battleground and find the path of growth. Being a teenager does not mean it is impossible to develop wisdom. Wisdom simply means making good choices using available knowledge and understanding. Wisdom equal to that of someone with twenty-five or fifty years more experience is not expected of a teen. However, like older adults, a teen can face differences of opinion with the exercise of a little wisdom that chooses self-control.

Wisdom seeks respectful conciliation of opposing points of view. Jesus calls it *peacemaking* in the Beatitudes. Wisdom turns away from obviously disrespectful actions and words, including all sarcasm. Wisdom determines to show respect even as the person holding an opposing viewpoint grabs at disrespect for a weapon. The instruction from Jesus on personal interactions is wisdom for any adolescent or adult to use.

Spirit-life takes on exceptional and vital meaning at this juncture. The path of life at the natural level often leads to tension and an urge to lash out verbally or even fight. That is the way of the old nature. Verbal or physical fighting with someone over opposing opinions is a negative spiritual path. Choosing the way of Jesus means forbearance in a passion-filled moment and de-escalation. The positive spiritual path redirects tense emotions and embraces conciliation (Prov 15:1).[1] As a believer in union with the Holy Spirit, a teen is capable of this redirect. The new nature in Christ is always able to choose the way of Christ. This is putting in order the inner being, who then works to bring order in the relationship.

Seeking to control personal emotions and pursue conciliation does not always resolve the oppositions from another person. Understand that opposition and conflict generated toward you from others may exist for reasons other than conflict over points of view. The emotional bent of a few folks toward negative, aggressive social interactions is an additional

---

1. Paraphrases adapted from the New American Standard Bible: ©2020 by the Lockman Foundation.

challenge. Make every effort, then disengage without reconciliation if necessary (Rom 12:18).

In a society prone to anger live the folks who upon hearing your opinion will respond with rancorous rhetoric devoid of empathy. Let the insult go. This individual demonstrates immaturity and impure motives by attacking with words on the basis of discovering your perspective on a topic. The passion of these individuals is human, but the negative direction of their behavior is uncivil. Incivility fosters anger, and anger disorders everyday life.

Anger leading to aggressiveness is not limited to a particular side of ideological or religious content; for example, both Republican and Democratic-aligned individuals may express opposition with disrespectful and ugly words. Similarly, people claiming Christianity or atheism may speak from a disordered emotional state and use an attacking tone carrying harsh words. The ironic tragedy in such cases is the combative person often justifies anger and aggression based on a perceived higher moral order.

Order in society is needed. In yet another conundrum of the human condition, we find people will erupt from disordered emotions seeking control of society ostensibly to supply order. Laws are intended to stabilize social interactions and enable all to seek well-being free from harm and unfairness. Establishing law and order through democratic consensus aims for obedience by the citizenry as a benefit for all.

Our individualistic culture often resists obedience to authority and social conventions like courtesy and deference. Broadly, our culture inculcates through the media and educational system an understanding that adults will self-direct and master their own fate through determination and discipline. I believe this, as well. However, that basic premise results in masses of self-actualized individuals, whose determination lacks compassion and weakens social bonds.

As a Christian, I accept God's redemptive plan for his creation standing on the simple acknowledgment that he is good. He is not just another being. He is our Creator and vastly superior to us. Therefore, the plan and its expectation of learning obedience to him are good. Profoundly for us humans, obedience to him is the only source of goodness. When I engage the society based on consideration for others, I am not only in obedience to God, but I am a builder of civility and that helps maintain a peaceful order. Yes, *Mister Rogers' Neighborhood* is still worth viewing.

Obedience to the Lord God begins with the simple act of acknowledging our need, a child-like state before him—a paradigm of this life is that humans are children spiritually even while adults in the material existence. A person of any age accepts obedience to God by finding in the new heart experience a desire to embrace his goodness and overcome the old nature human selfishness. The Bible calls it laying aside the old nature of selfishness and putting on the new nature, alive through God's divine nature. Thus, the believer discovers the capability and desire to manifest selflessness, compassion, and love of the highest order (Col 3:5–13).

I mention all this to help you understand that obedience to God is not robbing you of choice. On the contrary, it is the supreme choice of living the best, most humane life possible. The journey of obedience is a choice seeking the holistic development of a completed, godly humanity. I think of it described in the Bible as ". . . work out your salvation with fear and trembling" (Phil 2:12).

Additionally, being in Christ secures your eternal destiny. It is self-determination seeking a status woven into the story that God authors for his creation: his story (history, eh?) is that his creation is good (Gen 1:31); his creation is attacked by an enemy; this results in the death of the in-the-spirit life on earth (Gen 2:17). The created image bearer loses the image of God. God initiates a birthing of his image inside the hollowed shells of human beings by inserting himself back into humanity through Mary giving birth to Jesus (Luke 1:26–35); Jesus pays the price of the redemption for humanity dying in our stead for sinfulness (Mark 15:22–39). All humanity is invited to choose the Spirit-of-God life, his restoration of the original intent offered through the sacrifice of Jesus (Titus 2:11–14).

The in-spirit life, the abiding in the spirit of Jesus's life, begins with obedience in response to the message of the Gospel (John 15). That is the good news message: eternal life and a framework for humanity as God's image acquired through Jesus. He is the embodiment of the Spirit in which there is no hating of others, nor lust, nor harm (John 3:16–17). Regeneration continues through a growing relationship with the Father and the Son, Jesus, and we are supported in this obedience by the Holy Spirit.

Thinking practically, many expressions of Christian faith frame obedience as doing the specific commands written in the Bible. Certainly, these commands exist. Commands to love one another or to assist the poor or abstain from all lascivious behavior come to mind. Life is lived in real time: events around us; people speaking or acting toward us; decision-making concerning the level and tone of our involvement; and endless other open-ended situations are a daily challenge. Open-ended situations roll over us, wave after wave. The pressure is on. Responses precipitate the direction and tenor of what happens next. Therein lies the need for a mature mettle in the spirit.

Obedience is more than keeping specific commands of the written Word (Matt 23:13–26; Col 2:8–23). A developed in-the-spirit maturity emotionally moves the will to obedience. Our obedience in any moment to his Spirit produces the exercise of self-control. We move through open-ended situations in the best possible direction when our goal is obedience to the Holy Spirit. Love, joy, peace, patience, kindness, goodness, faithfulness, gentleness and self-control are powerful for effecting good results in all circumstances. Obedience inwardly to the peace and love of Jesus produces fruit of the spirit. It isn't hard to understand that a lack of being in the spirit, results in the old nature inserting falsehoods of hate, anxiety, pride, greed and more into our thoughts.

Obedience to God orders our emotions, inspires our imagination to purity, guides our intellectual assessments of truth and reality in the material realm, and supplies our deepest psychological needs. Go for it! Live this holy relationship with God the Father as a regenerated-in-Jesus human being. We believers will grapple with direct opposition from culture-based spiritual challenges. Be unafraid and resolute. Ultimately, the Christian learning submission to the still, small voice of God and choosing obedience moment by moment leads to the full, humane life of an overcomer.

P is for Purpose to Profess
Profanity, Pain, Perseverance

AMONG ACQUAINTANCES AND FRIENDS at school, cuss words may fly when teachers are out of earshot. You may have engaged in this behavior personally. I used foul language regularly before dedicating my life to Christ. In short, cussing is complaining on steroids, and there is no need to succumb to social expectations and pick up this unregenerated habit.

The word *cuss* is a shortened form of *curse* and such speech expresses harsh criticism or rejection of a person, object, or experience. Cursing someone is a profane act. *Profane*, like many words has several nuanced meanings. Overall, the variations might be summed up as contempt for something sacred.[1] For Christians, sacredness is all that God is: his works, commands, principles. *Profanity* is a derivative of *profane* and a synonym of *curse*, usually altered to *cuss*.[2] To cuss another human intends to damage or decry the worthiness of that person. Often, any use of profanity or curse words intends a powerful sense of negative feeling, the speaker gives little thought to profaning the holiness of God or his created humanity. The spirit behind curses against people or circumstances does not emanate from God, however; and whatever is not from him, is against him.

In our culture, cuss words are often considered normal, even expected depending on the group. When experiencing sudden physical pain, such as a searing burn, a knife blade slicing the skin, or a bruising fall, humans often react with a grimace and a loud expletive. These reactions range from euphemisms like *dang* and *shoot* to more vulgar words that are best left unmentioned.

---

1. Merriam-Webster's, *profane*, 930.
2. Merriam-Webster's, *curse* and *cuss*, 285–286.

What is the spiritual impact on our internal being when we use expletives? Let us consider two specific questions: Why do we curse; and is cursing effective speech? In observing day-to-day human expression, I surmise several reasons why profanity is used:

- group identification, an us-identity reinforced by common language choice, aka peer pressure;
- for emphasis—particularly in complaints;
- as a mark of independence from or rebellion against the norm;
- to mask fear behind a power facade;
- to emotionally justify an opinion when meaningful knowledge is weak;
- an appearance of power when control of circumstances does not exist; or
- as bluster to overwhelm the opinion of others.

Is cursing effective speech? No. Cursing language assumes a more powerful impact is carried by the language choice, but that power is a spiritual illusion. The power in a curse word is a falsehood. Seeking life in false pretenses, the speaker is reinforcing the old nature's weakness, a very negative impact.

Imagine two water fountains. From the first one flows cloudy, foul-smelling water. The one next to it provides fresh, clear spring water. Which would you choose? The evident foul smell and visual lack of purity warn a thirsty individual not to drink. Which fountain draws people?

Our speech is a utility function of the brain. Reading or calculating figures are processes of brain function. The brain is a tool. The brain generates an unending flow of cognition, evaluation, mental pictures of the natural world around us, and then synthesizes our imagination, creativity, and desires to initiate actions. We label this continuous, multifaceted mental flow as the *stream of consciousness*, which is a direct function of our composite inner self.

Sudden pain, whether physical or emotional, often unleashes an uncontrollable impulse overriding inhibitions, values, or intellectual filters. Pain momentarily commandeers the will. The emotional reaction is likely to be pejorative speech. In this spiritual eruption, profanities thrive, if one's will has already accepted a false belief in the vitality of a curse. Over time, habitual profanity embeds itself in the stream of consciousness as spiritual dissonance and manifests in speech as flotsam in a polluted river. The outward expression is evidence of one's inward spiritual condition (Luke 6:45).[3]

I do not condemn anyone who, in anger, frustration, or by habit, uses profanity or euphemisms for profanity. Instead, I write to foster understanding of the false sense of power in profane speech. Be equipped, dear reader beloved by God, with a spiritual insight into the purity of the indwelling Holy Spirit. An undisciplined and mismanaged will is the selfish center of the unregenerated human being, the old nature. Pursuing the spiritual life available through the indwelling Holy Spirit is an ongoing lesson in gaining control of one's will. This is part of the wonder of Christian spirit-life.

As our emotional and cognitive consciousness rests in the Presence of the Holy Spirit (details of resting in the R chapter), the fullness of the triune God supplies us in real time with control to accept or reject what crosses our stream of consciousness. Gaining control of the inner being produces control of the outward person.

Growing in any area of the spirit-life builds our understanding of spiritual processes. We learn navigating the tension between our basic human frailty (selfish desires) and God's supply (His Spirit). This is the reality of maturing emotionally. Practicing self-discipline over any aspect of being is a function of our own will. I use gaining control over language as a simple and practical way of learning and exercising the new creature's communion with the indwelling Presence of the Lord. Walking in the spirit is a learned understanding of being indwelt by the Holy Spirit. It is a practice that needs a practical starting place. How do we gain spirit knowledge? Use the real world circumstances at hand.

Jesus taught us to pray, ". . . deliver us from evil" (Matt 6:13). The *evil* from which we need deliverance is, first and foremost, the reckless and damaging selfishness that makes us prone to attitudes of irritation, frustration, impatience, or related anger rising within us toward others. If our purpose is to embrace love from God and give love to others, then our emotional states of irritation, impatience, and more in response to others is an emotional profaning of holy principle and the command to love others.

The sin of being unloving toward others roots in a spiritual failure to find replacement emotional responses for the old nature's adverse reactions.

---

3. Paraphrases adapted from the New American Standard Bible: ©2020 by the Lockman Foundation.

Monitoring, recognizing, and redirecting our negative reactions to people is the fulfillment of the command to love others through the in-indwelling Presence of Christ. As a Christian, such self-awareness disciplines word choice even in our thoughts. We take a willful action to seek out who we are in the Holy Spirit instead of being who we are naturally. Controlled speech is more than abstinence from curses; control also leads to developing speech full of grace, edification and encouragement. Don't think that is a bar too high. Rather, see that we live in him to find and be on the highest bar knowable by a human being.

The commands to love God, then others as ourselves, require this faith experience. Christian teaching on the practical development of faithful perseverance in loving others with supernatural power is sometimes skewed. From the pulpit, the sermon exhorts that our Christian life is supernatural. Yet, the practical nuts and bolts of immersion in a supernatural inward life—call it the *God connection*—suffers from sectarian bias. This weakens the consensus of understanding of walking with God Christians might otherwise experience.

The spiritual life depicted herein is a developing journey. This journey follows some basics: spiritual belief found and held, spirit lessons learned, comprehension of the inner being furthered, and exercise over the inner world producing the full fruit of the Holy Spirit. Our new creature within lives in a way the old nature is totally incapable of accomplishing. Yet, the new creature does not begin in a fully mature state by virtue of its birth at the moment of conversion to faith in Jesus. The process of maturation in spirit is an on-going learning function. Regeneration, or the kindling of the love, right-living, and a resulting joy within, is our Creator's intent for every convert. It is both process and point of the journey through life.

The new creature grows as we appropriate God's grace to support our journey into spiritual maturity. He is the Author and Finisher of our faith and the redemption of all humanity from sin. Thus, everything described herein stands on the goodness and grace of God. However, converts have a responsibility before him. The exertion of the will toward God and his righteousness moves one into a more profound spiritual experience. In other words, your responsibility is learning to think, decide, and act within the Holy Spirit.

Across a lifetime, a Christian will experience challenges to his or her faith. These will include challenging confrontations from non-Christians, personal circumstances that press one to deny their faith, government resistance and even harassment, family members turning their backs, and other scenarios. In all these, the biblical instruction is that we persevere in our faith. How does a believer maintain faith in the heat of oppression, repression, and rejection due to faith? We learn to stand against all opposition to faith.

Obedience to God is first and foremost our willing submission to the Holy Spirit's guidance and a receiving of peace through his comfort. We are then equipped by the Master for all spiritual battles. Ephesians 6:10–16 describes the Armor of God. Therein we read the "shield of faith" is used to "extinguish the flaming arrows of the evil one." We can rephrase those ancient words using interpretive, contemporary language for a faith-shield deflecting the flaming arrows of the enemy as follows: reading the Word develops one's understanding of faith, which builds desire and fuels the will to resist pride or fear stirred in the old nature by the god of this world.

By similar interpretive mechanism, other statements drawn from the Armor of God description in Ephesians include:

- the loins or waist wrapped in truth implies gut-level emotions find safe expression by following the truth of God's Word;
- a breastplate of righteousness describes how right(eous) choice-making is a strength to emotional stability;
- our feet shod in the gospel of peace indicate that wherever we walk, the humble announcement and active illustration of the peace of God arrives;
- and wearing a helmet of salvation assures that our intellectual understanding of all order and reality is protected against false assertions of any kind from any source.

The core reality of our daily life as Christians is seeking the kingdom of God first and above all else. We enter the kingdom by God's grace and purpose to learn an abiding trust in the Presence of Jesus within us. If we profess belief in Jesus and his saving grace unto salvation, then let our profession, all our speaking, be authentically spoken in a grace-filled purity that reflects Christ.

Are you thinking, *Simple to say, but . . .*? Read on.

Q is for Quantum Entanglement
Query, Qualify, Quest

A YOUTH BECOMING AN adult faces years of instruction and developing experiences. Does it seem to you that education has defined your life experience to date, and it may never end? Being an effective adult requires education. An effective education requires active, experiential participation. Learning experiences are designed for the classroom. The world beyond the classroom delivers learning in waves of circumstances, serendipitous to earth-quaking. An adult lamenting the challenges of being that adult might be heard to say, "I learned that in the school of hard knocks."

The individuals who effectively master adulthood are the people who accept responsibility for both lifelong learning and holistic human understanding. It takes both to become an agent instead of a victim. To achieve that better adult status, you must weave one other facet into the opportunity mix called life-learning; beyond education and experience, the authentic agent practices *meaningful reflection*.

A person replacing random emotional reactions with proactive, self-disciplined responses honed by reflective practice flourishes with emotional maturity. Reflection over choices that connects one's core values to life applications clarifies and deepens self-awareness. A sharpened self-awareness supplies insight that shapes and strengthens volition. A non-Christian may discover, practice, and grow from self-reflection. For the Christian, it is the God-ordained path of abiding in the Spirit of Christ. What difference is there then between the two people if both benefit from reflective practice? The difference is the outcomes achieved. The non-Christian's agency is limited to one individual's success in the ways of the world. The authentic Christian is growing in the wisdom of the Eternal God in preparation for a resurrection to eternal life.

Effective reflection stands on strong questioning skills. All learning, including emotional, is informed and strengthened by asking questions. In one browser search (questioning the digital data library), I found:

- "The three question strategies . . . "
- "The four essential questions . . . "
- "The five types of questions in grammar . . . "
- "The six modes of questions (proposed by Socrates)"
- "The seven types of research questions . . . "
- "The fifteen types of questions . . . "

You get the idea—thoughtful inquiry utilizes multiple ways of questioning. The efficacy of the self-reflective query must differentiate the categories of questioning. This is logical since learning experiences process new information by understanding across intellectual, emotional, and physical capacities, and these are built from varying motivations.

Personal authenticity materializes like alloys of metal. The characteristics of the ingredient ores forge together forming a singular, characteristic strength. Christian agency emerges in the heart, when multiple motivations find a harmony of action. The reflective query is a forge within the inner being. The wonder of the Christian experience is the Presence of the Lord Jesus moderating the reflective process.

As a believer in the revelation of Jesus as the Messiah, the pursuit of spiritual maturity starts, moves through, and stands on Bible reading. Learning effective questioning of Scripture facilitates learning the way of spirit-life. We question the Scripture as children of God and as students yearning to grasp a providential understanding of our journey on Earth. Reflective practice examines our motives, our outward actions, and the outcomes of our choices against the light of truth, the Scriptures. The power of the reflective process is the guidance and comfort from the Presence of God within.

Two stipulations of Scripture interpretation are the imperatives guiding how we handle the Bible. One directive is that content be interpreted in context. The second is that no interpretation can be outside of or violate the whole of biblical revelation. We must interpret any scriptural precept by what is written around it, and the interpretation must maintain harmony with the big-picture revelation of the Bible. In these two hermeneutic principles, we find the understanding needed for applications producing actions true to the righteousness of God's Presence. An excellent book instructing on interpretive principles is *Hermeneutics: Principles and Processes of Biblical Interpretation,* by Henry A. Virkler.

In my view (other Christians may hold a different opinion), there is a logical place in Scripture fundamental to embarking on the reflective process. Jesus' prayer for his followers in John 17 is the starting point for experiencing the truth revealed in the Bible. Jesus prayed for us—all those who commit to him as disciples—to be one with him and the Father. I am certain his prayers are answered! Seek to understand what oneness with the Father means as it is central to living within God's plan.

Responsible interaction with the Heavenly Father includes building Bible knowledge, a commitment to engaging in prayer, and the active, reflective process supporting ongoing spiritual maturity. If the Holy Spirit is given for guidance and comfort, then growth in our spirit being as it aligns with that Presence is basic, essential, and practical.

In meaningful reflection, we learn to use qualitative data. How can qualitative data, subjective in its interpretation, be trusted to reveal the truth? The subjective nature of qualitative data requires carefulness in making evaluations of truth, but abandoning qualitative analysis because of the subjectivity involved is an error. Quantitative analysis is limited to the material world, and therefore, it has limited utility for developing spiritual growth. Think about it. Does measuring and recording physical reality, the quantifying of the observable, provide anyone with the full understanding of being human? Can love be reduced to quantifying details? No. Therefore, we must use qualitative information to understand the totality of the human experience. Four categories of qualitative questions may be logically considered for this purpose:

- of the Scriptures to gain understanding of spirit-life in the Lord;
- of society in differentiating positive and negative influences;
- of ourselves as participants in the kingdom of God and the culture around us;
- of the Holy Spirit who sustains us with guidance and comfort.

Ask spiritual questions that seek a fair evaluation of the reasons, methods, or motivations behind all behaviors. This type of questioning aims to foster spiritual growth, in contrast with asking for a different outward behavior by fiat of God. For example, do not ask for patience as if it is doled out one scoop at a time. Patience naturally fruits from the Holy Spirit's Presence. Believing in the indwelling Holy Spirit, ask how to connect with his patience available within through his Presence. Ask for insight into the triggers of your impatient feelings and thoughts. Ask to be taught his way of patience.

Perhaps you question the reliability of the Bible itself. The Bible is supported by quantitative data from science, history, and archaeology, but that is beyond the scope of this writing. I recommend reading the book *Is Atheism Dead,* by Eric Metaxas. It provides a great starting point for researched, quantitative support of the Bible's veracity.

In my experience, the Bible provides the most compelling qualitative analysis of spiritual existence. I have studied or observed a variety of religious and spiritual traditions including voodoo, witchcraft, spiritualism, Buddhism, ancestor worship, Taoism, Hindu polytheism, and the three major monotheistic religions: Judaism, Christianity, and Islam. I grew up in an agnostic home. As an adult, I embraced atheism for four years. Nothing explains our collective history or the emotional state of humanity as profoundly as the Bible. The qualitative data of what is taught by the Bible about truth, love, and goodness is beyond comparisons to the spiritual alternatives.

Two common phrases heard within Christian circles are used in this work, "walking with God" and "life in the spirit." These two phrases are synonymous in meaning the inner life developed after the second birth. Spiritual experiences characteristic of walking with God are depicted through biblical stories and delineated by instructive Scripture. The God connection is the greatest quest for any human, which unfolds by reading biblical, qualitative data. A partial list includes:

- the gain of intellectual insight into absolute truth;
- the receiving his Holy Spirit within one's soul;
- maturation of the heart from the practice of sacrificial love;
- guidance by the Holy Spirit into the power of compassion and loving-kindness;
- the fullest expression of human life;
- strength for faith in an unseen reality; and
- equipping by the living God against the spiritual oppression inherent in a world system ruled by the god of rebellion.

Q is for Quantum Entanglement

Consider Matthew 5:8 in the Beatitudes, "Blessed are the pure in heart, for they shall see God." Asking qualitative questions here would explore the nature of a pure heart and analysis of one's personal experience of purity. The revealed answer in the Bible is that purity from God is imputed to us by the Atonement through Jesus; from this foundational intervention by God's grace, we learn the choosing of purity in thought and action. That choice is a practical, material world exercise of in-the-spirit reality. See the intersection? The consequences of choosing pure thoughts alters the perception of self and others and thus impacts the actions we take.

To walk with God alters our whole being. John 1:4 says, "He (Jesus) was the life, and the life was the light of all men." The life of God in us, a light within our being, is restored in the born-again state. The spiritual rebirth begins by seeing Jesus as truth. The sight with the "eyes of the heart" is described in Ephesians 1:18. His life becomes the direct source of our inner life, and the spirit vision grows.

Each human on earth senses within something of the majesty of God, a remnant of the whole person God wrought in Creation but was lost due to the fall. Ephemeral feelings surface, and the natural human senses this remnant image of God imprinted on all humanity. We call these feelings many things: the fire in the belly; a call from destiny; an inherent drive to soar; and other wordings attempting to explain a deep sense of eternal purpose. Many build from these feelings an optimism for personal greatness. From this inner-drive mechanism springs the desire for an *epic quest* as fulfillment of one's life. The epic quest is a thematic mainstay of literature across cultures past and present.

False religions and other misdirected spiritual belief systems stem from this inner sense of greatness. In religious teaching, the epic quest often reduces to a-carrot-and-stick mentality. The carrot is an improved personal goodness which appeals to an inner sense of greatness. The stick ever holding the carrot just beyond reach is the expectation for behaving by the rules as stipulated by a religious system. Likewise, in atheistic social reformation (humanism), the carrot is the quest to produce a better world, and the stick is conformity to humanistic ideals.

Authentic Christianity rejects both of these responses to our innate sense of destiny. The anointed of God, the Christ, whom we accept and serve as the one true God, is the gateway to a whole new being. In an authentic Christian experience, the born-again believer is enabled to reflect and effect God's goodness. We do not do good to make the world a better place. We become one with Ultimate Goodness and experience the promise of creation while living as an alien within the tumult of sin rampant in society. We do not gain a great destiny but accept a place within God's dominion over earth. Thereby, we embrace the sense of greatness by entering the intent of the Lord in creation as a regenerated human bearing his image.

The complete and contented human is *only* the result of fulfillment in the Lord God. All three parts of being, heart-mind-body, find meaning and purpose through the Presence of Jesus within us. His inherent wisdom and knowledge are known and accessed by faith in the promise of his indwelling Presence.

Like the physics of quantum entanglement, our life is in Christ seated at the right hand of God, and Christ in us is our life on earth (Col 3:1).[1] We are a particle connected to God; "we live and move and have our being in him" (Acts 17:28). Choosing our actions based on understanding his goodness, the Holy Spirit empowers and lifts us. In our actions, we reveal a reflection of who God is to others. We find our identity through him. God is love, and godliness exhibited as love results from the quest for growth and maturation in spirit. We can do this.

---

1. Paraphrases adapted from the New American Standard Bible: ©2020 by the Lockman Foundation.

R is for Righteousness
Rights, Religion, Rest

The Civil Rights Act of 1964 became law, and the segregated Southern society of my youth cracked wide open. A culture stipulated and maintained by Jim Crow laws became illegal. The U.S. society I knew vectored toward a new horizon. Our city government closed the public pool rather than integrate it. I was eight years old and realized I could care less about the color of anyone's skin. I wanted to swim no matter who swam alongside me.

The civil rights movement and resulting legislation of 1964 shine as a morally-demanded political turn, a righteous step for our country. Until Congress acted in 1964, the southeastern states maintained by force of law a fearsome discrimination against African-Americans. Additionally to the South's legislated and enforced segregation, African-Americans citizens across the United States faced discrimination and societal disenfranchisement. Other people groups were targeted for discrimination, as well; people of Asian and Latino ethnicity knew a painful and oppressive exclusion from full participation in society.

The concept of rights and privileges protected by law generates passionately held perspectives in U.S. culture. The current national discourse is filled with antithetical antagonisms labeled a *culture war*. This "war" is a diametrical opposition of ideologies expressed most clearly in the political labels *Left* and *Right*. The current estrangement between these two political perspectives roots in a profound shift of spiritual emphasis within our nation since WW ll. That shift relegated the in-place Judeo-Christian heritage of Western Civilization as the core of U.S. identity to a reduced status of just another religion in a secular society. Boil the history down to the spiritual-philosophical forces at play, and our current national argument stems from opposing views on the meaning and experience of human biological sex.

In both literal and figurative terms, sex is a vital topic. (Sexuality is addressed specifically in the next chapter.) For Christians, who accept that Jesus is God and understand ourselves as aliens waiting for his established government on earth, a more significant issue than personal rights is righteousness. Righteousness is a common topic in Christian teaching and refers to personal choices based on God's moral standards. Righteousness as a concept is questioned, even sneered at, by many outside the Body of Christ.

There are two reasons non-Christians may denigrate righteousness. Due to some Christians' moral failures, outside observers may logically construe a doubting cynicism toward Christian faith practices. A second motive for expressing cynicism may germinate from a desire to undermine the idea of righteousness. If the concept of righteousness can be debunked as false, the speaker may feel absolved of any responsibility for their unrighteousness. There are two general issues within Christian experience that generate cynical derision from non-Christians: immature attitudes of believers and moral failure, particularly among leaders, fueling an assumption all Christians are hypocrites.

Self-righteousness will often link with spiritual immaturity. Self-righteousness lacks humility and leads to devaluing people outside the faith for their perceived sinfulness. Self-righteousness often flourishes in congregations where immature leadership upholds standards first and foremost intent on the management and control of church members. Mature Christianity rejects legalism. True righteousness transcends legalism and is the natural fruit of abiding in the Holy Spirit of Jesus. Humility chosen within the Presence will not identify personal choices as earning any favor from the Father, and looks upon all sins of selfishness in any believer with mercy first and continually. As Jesus said, we should forgive sins seventy times seven times (Matt 18:22).[1]

Righteousness is not a moving target but a God-ordained standard. Believers, however, are at varied stages in developing their reliance on righteousness as a conscience-guided choice applied through submission to the Holy Spirit's direction. Paul alludes to this in Ephesians 4:15, ". . . speaking the truth in love, we are to grow up in all aspects into him who is the head, even Christ."

The label of hypocrisy follows moral failures by Christians and particularly those of Christian leaders. To call all such failure hypocritical lacks

---

1. Paraphrases adapted from the New American Standard Bible: ©2020 by the Lockman Foundation.

understanding and insight concerning the growth and maturation of the new being. We all sin even after becoming a Christian and claiming to be born again (1 John 1:8). Nonetheless, high profile leaders who choose sin and attempt to hide it should expect exposure and high profile notoriety as a consequence (Gal 6:7).

Discussions spotlighting the sinfulness of humans will often stir a non-believer to rebuff or rebuke the message of purity of the heart available in the regeneration in Christ. Non-believers often denounce any Christian stance on righteous behavior—particularly when so many leaders in the church make headlines for immorality. The non-believer generally asserts that all behavior stems from personal identity and related choices. This position rationalizes Christian delineation between old and new natures is not reasonable nor possible. By rejecting Christian understanding of sin, the non-believer adopts an intellectual position without moral boundaries, and thus finds freedom to consider personal choice as the only standard needed.

A second justification by non-believers for behavior that Christians label as sin is that individual liberty is authorized by constitutional rights. Personal rights are held in high regard, even with a type of reverence, among U.S. citizens. Most U.S. citizens will recognize and many can quote Thomas Jefferson from the Declaration of Independence,

> "We hold these truths to be self-evident, that all men are created equal, that they are endowed by their Creator with certain unalienable rights, and that among these are life, liberty, and the pursuit of happiness."[2]

What constitutes happiness divides our social fabric these days. Common choices of contemporary society justified as the pursuit of happiness include promiscuity, same-sex marriage, and abortion. A non-Christian, amoral worldview accepts much behavior that Christians must reject if living faithfully within the teachings of Scripture.

The important catchphrase is "living faithfully within the teachings of Scripture." We Christians are human and fail the standards we often espouse. It is understandable why anyone practicing sin as a normal facet of life resents the seeming hypocrisy of Christians who act immorally while describing societal culture as immoral. The purpose of this book is the development and maintenance of a God-honoring lifestyle discovered

---

2. Jefferson, "The Declaration of Independence."

in and dependent on the supply of faithfulness and self-control found in the spirit. The source of right choices is the will submitted to living in the Spirit of Christ.

Christianity draws much scorn for the immoral, selfish decisions by Christians in the historical record and within our current culture. The Crusades, Inquisition, slave trade are some examples of historic Christian religion causing harm and suffering. In this century, financial fraud and sexual immorality of Christian leaders consistently arrive in news headlines. It is clear that immorality exists and is sometimes perpetrated by those who espouse Christian faith. Why? Moral failure lies with individuals, not with the revelation of God or his goodness. Profession of faith is one aspect of Christianity. Living faithfully is a process of learning to think and feel in new ways. People failing the lessons does not mean the lessons were ill-conceived. That individuals fail the morality they profess only underscores the human need for God's work of salvation to be completed.

The absoluteness of God requires learning what righteousness means to him and how we may live in it. Our righteousness is a much bigger issue than earthly rights. Personal rights as a U.S. citizen flicker by as part of a temporary and brief state of living inside our material body. Righteousness through the atonement of Christ and learning to overcome the sin nature is part of the eternal story of God and his creation.

Righteousness sounds like religion's command, but it is better understood as a spiritual state. Tying righteousness to religious practice can obscure the word's meaning. Righteousness is the right way of all within God's order. Finding and understanding our spiritual place in the Holy Spirit is the only authentic Christian moral direction. Our interactions with others are effective and righteous when ordered within the standard of the Father. Right-ordering, or righteousness, requires being enlivened by the Holy Spirit, and that requires we know how to rest in God rather than depend on ourselves.

The corrupt nature with which we are born, despite our heritage as the creation of God, must be addressed. Enter the sacrificial Lamb of God, the Son, who allowed himself to be judged for all sin. His righteousness and purity supplant one's sinful nature. With our imperfect selfishness before God forgiven, an act of grace from God ensues: our new birth of spirit. The new spirit is a new source and direction for our expression of righteousness as a human. The state of humanity as lived in Eden before deception brought the death of the spirit is restored to the here and now. The road to a new life is opened to the believer, but the world remains in its fallen state. We must live here during the time of waiting on Jesus to return. We face the challenge of refusing the knowledge of good and evil, that is, knowing what living in unrighteousness feels like. We learn to live in life, the abiding in Jesus, who is the Tree of Life (Gen 2:16–17). We must learn to be overcomers of sin.

All human endeavor mixes the good and bad of humanity, including the development of Christian religions. Christians fail righteousness for two reasons: there is a learning curve in becoming mature in spirit; and Christian religions fail clear teaching on the mechanism that enables righteousness as a consistent choice, the union with God.

Christian religion emerged and embedded with Western Civilization over the last 2,000 years. Religious traditions were established, splintered, and synthesized into new offshoots throughout its history. Please hear no condemnation of anyone by these words. I am evaluating the impact of human efforts to live out the faith. After the last two millennia, Christian teaching remains diverse regarding the application of God's absolute truth as revealed in the Bible. Dogmas within various denominational teachings do not promote the maturation of the new being. In fact, dogmatic assumptions based on a specific interpretation of Scripture may hinder spiritual growth.

We need Christian fellowship, teaching, and prayer. We Christians also need to participate in designated gatherings, as they are essential to our new life in the Spirit of Jesus. However, religious rites and traditions that merely remind us of scriptural teachings will not accomplish the maturation of our spirit being. Does true faith exist within denominational practices? Of course! God's work within anyone's heart reaches inside man-made boundaries. The distinction between congregants walking in faith and those merely practicing religious dogma lies within the heart. The difference is between those who trust the Father and those who trust in traditions.

Which denomination is best for understanding and fully practicing righteousness? Righteousness is not in following traditions based on Scripture. Is the atonement alone sufficient for salvation? Certainly, in the sense that our salvation is not earned and must be based on the righteousness of God placed by Jesus between us and the Father. Yet, repeatedly stating the truth that our righteousness is imputed, while doing nothing to develop practical knowledge of Jesus manifesting in the believer, is to trust dogma over faith.

Christianity reduced to the recitation of prayers and seasonal Bible verses is mere words without the power of authentic purity. Call being faithful to practice traditions *religiosity*. It is a powerless form. Those greedy and immoral leaders making headlines were excellent in keeping the appearance of conformity to traditions, but they must not have fully died to the fallen nature. Therein lies the problem of Christian failure to maintain righteousness. To walk in obedience and live choosing righteous behavior, we actively pursue humility before the Father. We accept the guidance of the Holy Spirit. This is a state of being accessible only to the regenerated human. We seek, knock, and ask for understanding the authentic words and actions governed by compassion, kindness, humility, gentleness, and patience resident within us by the Holy Spirit (Col 3:12). As well, we discover the power of the regenerated will to move in mercy and justice while renouncing by choice the greed, lust, hatred, and malice of a spirit-dead humanity (Mic 6:8).

In knowing the Father through the work of Jesus Christ, we place no hope in rights granted or denied through earthly citizenship or the mandates of tradition in historic religious practice. We set our heart, mind, and strength on the Word of God, written and delivered through the miracle of the Bible, which instructs and reveals our supernatural experience of the Living Word, the Holy Spirit within us. Our hope is built on nothing less.

We die to selfishness and live to offer back to the Lord all intellectual skill and physical prowess. Excelling in the uses of mind and body are not for building confidence in the self nor satisfaction of worldly desires. We have died to self-esteem while God teaches us self-respect born of the love he showered on us in giving the Son to redeem us. An assignment of worth standing fully on his grace, love, and righteousness.

Linked with the dying-to-self paradigm is a second biblical descriptor with import on this discussion: entering God's Sabbath rest (Heb 4:7–9). It is a place of emotional rest, freed from the cares of sin, strife, and worry over the supply of material needs. This rest in God delivers a surprising discovery: in the Holy Spirit, peace becomes our confidence, and joy becomes our satisfaction. Peace and joy then come to us from knowing the rest in God, who is righteousness. The kingdom of God is righteousness, peace, and joy in the Holy Spirit (Rom 14:17).

S is for the Sacred Union
Sexuality, Sensuality, Spirit

By sophomore year in high school, U.S. students have encountered formal education on sexual reproduction in plant and animal species, including the human mammal. Likewise, all sophomores experience casual culture jokes, curiosity seeking, and sincere inquiry into human sexuality. Sexual reproduction is a part of life, and the changes in the body through puberty are the natural development of the reproductive organs. The increase in reproductive hormones stirs individual interest in this topic regardless of curriculum or peer influence.

Beyond the scope of the science of human reproduction, a broader discussion on human sexuality develops on the ethics and morals of sexual expression. The powerful human mechanism we label as the sex drive meshes body, heart, and mind focal points. It is primal within the loins, stirs vibrant links to the emotions, and twines through thought to distraction. It is a tiered stimulus impacting our interaction with people. This intrinsic wiring sways our perception of many situations and people. The influence of the sex drive may color as positive or negative one's overall reaction to another person. We often describe it metaphorically as a "fire" in the body. The desire for sexual intercourse is deeply tied to our spiritual well-being and carries with it a profound responsibility—the capacity to produce children.

An accepted cultural ethic placing sexual intercourse as only right within marriage ordered U.S. society and law roughly for the first 200 years of the nation. Individuals failed the moral standard, of course, across the spectrum of U.S. society. Yet, this identified human failure did not alter the general societal perception that sexual intercourse within marriage is both a moral order sanctioned by the Creator God and the source of wholesome family life.

The 1960s sexual revolution historically stands as a massive grassroots redress of established standards on sexual behavior that insisted sexuality should not be restricted by state or religion. The wave of change sweeping U.S. culture in the 1960s and 70s sought freedom from a societal expectation of lifetime commitment to one spouse.

The logic that justifies a no-commitment sexual experience builds from the belief that there is no Creator God. In this frame of logic, hormones and individual psyche govern the seeking of sexual union, and moral guidance is rejected. The marriage commitment prescribed in Scripture has experienced a rapid slide to the wayside of U.S. cultural consciousness. Many of your friends and older voices will describe cohabitation before marriage as a wise test of whether a relationship is worth a lifetime commitment. Additionally, never choosing to marry and being sexually active have gained widespread acceptance for sexual intercourse as merely an adult activity. Generally speaking, the contemporary person adhering to this secularism expects multiple relationships across a lifetime that include sexual intimacy.

I write to instruct and encourage your formation of understanding marriage and the sexual union of two people through the light of Jesus's directives on the subject. This topic is covered repeatedly in other books, both Christian and non-Christian, but the importance of the topic spurs a mention here, as well. Jesus gives two simple mandates: God created male and female to be joined in marriage commitment and having been joined in marriage, the two people are not to be separated (Matt 19: 4–6).[1] In these two stipulations, he indicates marriage is a heterosexual commitment, which the Creator intends to last for the entirety of their remaining life experience. The terms *male* and *female* are basic, biological references. The mandate for one lifelong relationship formed between two people of opposite sexes could not be more precise.

The logic for seeking a married-for-life experience and embarking on the same is rooted in Christian faith. The power of the logic rides on an active trust in the wisdom of the Bible on this topic. A monogamous, lifelong commitment to marriage is not just God's command; it is his design for ordering of life.

Fidelity to marriage will demand emotional work and spiritual perseverance. Maintenance of monogamy goes beyond believing in mere platitudes. The commitment required becomes a love built with one person

---

1. Paraphrases adapted from the New American Standard Bible: ©2020 by the Lockman Foundation.

across a lifetime. Fidelity and strength of love is no happy accident, nor is it a schmaltzy ending of a Hollywood romantic comedy.

The Lord would have his children experience a spiritual depth of love only discovered through the marriage covenant. Love from God is unconditional, long suffering, and ever-deepening. Christian marriage reflects his characteristics. It is a human metaphor illustrating the promise from God of his eternal covenant with those who belong to him. The monogamous marriage union between two people beautifully reflects Jesus' commitment to a group of people joined to him for eternity as the Bride of Christ.

An inherent emotional growth results from working on a relationship according to the instruction of Scripture. Committed love occurs within marriage as 1 Corinthians 13 instruction on love is practiced. Married love deepens as a function of the dedication of two hearts to manifest the highest value available to any human, love as defined by God. Paul identifies such love as the greatest human experience (1 Cor 13:11–13).

Young Christians and new converts of any age face challenges in the development and maintenance of sexual purity. Meeting the challenge successfully through the empowerment of the Holy Spirit drives maturity in loving God and others. Conversely, failure to embrace sexual purity increases selfishness and deadens the spiritual substance of overall goodness. Impatience, anxiety, and hardness of heart toward the Lord God and other humans will result from a lack of self-control over the sex drive.

Jesus refers to the practice of sexual intercourse outside marriage as fornication. God's acceptable marriage experience and all fornication share a common physical component: sensuality. Two applications of sensuality given by the dictionary illustrate our intellectual understanding of the term. First is the awareness of the pleasures we experience through our natural senses. For example, consider the delights found in aromas, flavors, beauty beheld, fine linens against skin, and all music. Sensuality sweeps across more than the enjoyment of our physical environment. These positive sensing experiences engage our emotions and stir desire to continue or repeat the experience. Desire complicates the sensual experience, and thus, we arrive at the second meaning of sensuality: the overindulgence in sensual pleasure.[2]

Sexual intimacy is the creation of the Father. He intends the one flesh experience go beyond physical enjoyment. This deep level intimacy secures our emotional identity. Conversely, multiple relationships over time wear away and break one's emotional identity.

---

2. Merriam-Websters, *sensuality*, 1067.

Scientific understanding of the body instructs on human reproductive capability. The culture surrounding us pushes the idea that all pleasure is good. However, our culture rejects God's instruction in Scripture on sensuality. The older you get, the more you will recognize that a significant number of people live strictly for sensual experiences. It is hard for many people to define and maintain reasonable limits against overindulgence. Eating flavorful food is enjoyable, and there is no sin in this enjoyment. The sensual desire for great-tasting food, ungoverned and undisciplined, may foment gluttonous habits, harming the body with excessive weight gain, and building attitudes of dissipation in the heart.

Identified human extremes and uncontrolled dominating characteristics of personality were previous topics. However, here, we scrutinize the inherent pleasure known when sharing bodies outside of marriage. The challenge to our understanding of this topic is the consistent force with which our culture promotes sensuality and related sexual behaviors, which the Bible defines as sin.

Lust is a natural emotional response stemming from our innate selfish nature in which we are born. Lust is a toxic mix of body hormones linked with a greedy, possessive factor. A common error is to identify satisfying one's lust as an acceptable fulfillment of our basic needs of attachment and pleasure/pain avoidance. Humans can delude themselves that lustful desire satisfied fulfills one's basic needs. As a result, we humans are prone to perceive lustful impulses as loving another person. Wanting and loving are two distinctly different concepts.

The absolute truth from God is that sin is the fruit of our innate spiritual condition from birth. Sexual sin is a pervasive trap for humans, damaging the heart, mind, and body. (If two married people remain faithful, they will never contract STDs.) An uncontrolled, unrestrained sexual drive leads deeper into the darkness of the supernatural realm. Such progression is a fundamental aspect of the spiritually-connected world we inhabit. Scripture clearly warns that sinful sexual behavior leads to total spiritual delusion about right and wrong (Rom 1: 18–32; 1 Cor 6:12–20).

There are two spiritual forces at work in this earthly reality: the Lord God, revealed by Jesus Christ, and his enemy, an evil force named Lucifer. Regardless of the moniker, this evil force intends to destroy all humans. Evil is the god of this world system. Every soul is spiritually inclined from birth towards physical gratification, self-aggrandizement, and the love of wealth.

S is for the Sacred Union

In such a soul, the wind of the spirit of the Antichrist shapes one's direction. (Luke 6:45; Matt 12:34).

Since the fall of humanity and into this age, attitudes and rationalizations produce war, greed, lust, and deceit; such are the fruit of the Antichrist spirit. The spirit of Christ leads in the understanding of true justice and compassion. There is refreshment for anyone and all within the living water, the spirit stream of Jesus.

The topic of spirits challenges our thinking. We are oriented to thinking in material terms. The wonder of God requires words to frame, reflect, and develop our understanding of the One who is spirit, love, and light. The words are not formless. Faith is informed, and love is instructed by them. The substance of faith then builds confidence. Insight into the spirit of God produces quality decisions and mature, acceptable actions in his eyes.

Across our culture in the twenty-first century, people involve themselves intimately without the commitment of marriage. The entertainment media promotes romantic surrealism depicting illicit affairs and licentiousness as love. All to the loss of understanding the benefit and security found in marriage.

A loving, committed family between two adults of the opposite sex is God's context for sexual intercourse. From that commitment, an emotional dynamic emerges that bountifully fulfills the attachment needs of a husband and wife. In God's plan, sexual intimacy is not the root of the love between two people; it is the flower.

As a married man of forty-four years and as a father and grandfather, I inform you of the power available to understand the complexities of a marriage relationship and to persevere in the marriage covenant. Faithful submission to the Holy Spirit within and faithful adherence to the love instructions of the Bible will establish a marriage for the long haul and secure a healthy family unit. Yes, marriage is inherently challenging, but its gain is the fulfillment of a God-ordained beauty unparalleled among those who live in the darkness perpetrated by the god of this world.

Pursue life in the spirit of Christ and avoid the counterfeits of lust and selfishness that masquerade as love. Spiritual maturity equips the believer with self-control to govern the hormonal drive. The fulfillment of the psychological needs for emotional intimacy and the physical drive for union with a spouse are both gifts the Father gives. Married life held onto and honored between two people across decades produces a union of incredible beauty and deep love. It is the sacred union of creation, male and female, the design of Lord God.

T is for Transforming Truth
Tradition, Thinking, Truth

JESUS CAME TO EARTH, walked among us, and taught the truth. The revelation he delivered spurs these words. His teachings recorded in the first four books of the New Testament document God pouring out his truth upon humanity, the truth lost in Eden. The absolute truth of the Lord guides the believer in developing sound judgment over all interpersonal relationships and interactions with the world's economic-political structure. Most significantly, the truth instructs one's ongoing management of the sense of self through the Holy Spirit. I invite your consideration of a perspective that calls you to developing maturity in the spirit in response to the Presence of the Spirit within you. All you need—what every human needs—is the truth.

The splintering of the Christian faith into tens of thousands of denominations worldwide evidences variations of Scripture interpretations scattered across the world. However, a common theme and consequential life response remains throughout those divisions: accept Jesus and walk in the Holy Spirit that he gives to the regenerated human. The Bible states there is one faith (Eph 4: 1–6).[1] Based on that revelation, across those thousands of denominations a few core beliefs are identifiable. The specific differences bared for view are varied conjectural interpretations pushed to the level of biblical authority that become cemented as tradition. The commonly held belief is the fullness of the gospel. The conjectures serve the purposes of those building power structures over others. A few of the groups follow their imagination too much and cults result.

Traditions have positive and negative consequences. On the positive side, a tradition reminds us of truths from the Word of God. For example,

---

1. Paraphrases adapted from the New American Standard Bible: ©2020 by the Lockman Foundation.

the nativity scene rendered annually at Christmas reminds us of the virgin birth and humble circumstances heralding God's coming to Earth as the prophesied Emmanuel. On the negative side, the practice of tradition frequently becomes routine and weakens the experience of the Presence of God within us. When the love and power of God are known through traditions that rarely motivate our day-to-day living, spiritual dullness and compromise with worldly desires ensue.

A Christian tradition cannot substitute for the Spirit of Christ in our hearts. With one's spiritual eyes focused on traditions, the heart grows hungry for something more substantive. Feeding the inner being on traditions instead of active trust in the Holy Spirit starves the heart. A starving heart is easily distracted by security worries or wealth gathering as important for satisfying the heart (Matt 13:22).

Pointing out the weakness of wealth as food for the heart does not imply that the Christian life of self-denial closes a door to what is accepted as quality living. We need to delineate the meaning of *quality*. The frame of reference here is vitally important. Think it through: Jesus warns that the way to destruction is broad, and the way of life is narrow. However, the words *broad* and *narrow* speak to the qualitative reality of spirit. What was Jesus qualitatively broadening versus narrowing regarding life as a human?

The dominating nature of evil pulls human motive, initiative, and productive capacity away from God. Thus Jesus labels as broad everything that we might seek materially to meet our needs (attachment, structure/order, self-enhancement and pleasure-gain/pain avoidance) when the material reality moves us away from reliance on God. Jesus narrows choices of material experiences that inherently contain false intellectual suppositions, body-titillating behaviors, and self-glorification. He thus delivers a narrowing mandate for living: separation from the broad range of rampant falsehoods promising fulfillment with counterfeit satisfactions.

Conversely, Jesus extends to those belonging to him the broad spiritual world of knowing and living within the abundance of the Father. Obedience to follow the narrow way rewards the believer with an opening of the inner being to the wealth of wisdom and knowledge available in God. Submission to the narrow way of Jesus releases the power of love, justice, understanding, and forgiveness from within us toward others. Obedience in this frame is the embrace of purity enabling godly love. Thus, Christians find abundance of spiritual life through the depth, breadth, length, and height of love only found in the Lord. This is transformative truth.

For the sake of discussion, let's divide *truth* into four levels of understanding: individual truth; cultural truth; universal truth; and absolute truth. The word *truth* is inconsistently used in conversation as speakers switch frames of reference between thoughts generated within these four categories. As measured by an individual, truth and experience are synonymous. Conjecture, opinion, and misunderstanding others are all woven within the "truth" of personal experience. Observations or conclusions are subjectively stated as personal truth. Individual truth is fraught with partial analysis and biased interpretation when disconnected from a reliable standard.

The broader idea of cultural truth involves a larger frame of reference than individually defined truth. As previously discussed, people develop within a shaping force of culture. The ideas and values believed and accepted by a shared-heritage group define one's cultural truth. These cultural beliefs forge a sense of established truths by multiplication across many minds and hearts.

The cultural take on values by U.S. citizens, thus the experience of culture-based truth, evolves on such divergent factors as increasing population, a varied array of perspectives comprising the voting constituency, corporations as influential stakeholders, progressing technology, the influence of the arts, and the longevity of the organized political structure. This evolution pressures the collective to define shared values and creates sharp disagreement about what is the truth.

A more significant challenge for defining truth grapples with ideas built from universal truth common to humans around the globe. Discussions of truth broaden and deepen when the power of emotions like love, hate, jealousy, tenderness, and familial commitment enter the analysis. These universal truths prompt a sincere inquiry into establishing order within a diverse population and fostering the best responses from as many individuals as possible. In other words, the search for truth at this level seeks the greatest good for all. Inquiry at this level will always confront whether an absolute truth capable of governing all thought exists.

Much debate currently occurs in this country over whether or not there is a Creator God. If no intelligent Creator is involved in the genesis of humankind, then there is no absolute truth. If there is no absolute truth, we must sift through the myriad of perspectives to determine what is best for a few hundred million people with whom we share the nation. If a Creator God exists, his declarations are the truth and satisfy the question, "What is truth?" This book flows from the premise that God exists as described in the Bible, and he is absolute truth. It is then logical to accept his statements and intentions for humans as the truth on which all intellectual thinking, decision-making, and actions turn. The nation will never do this. Individuals decide to believe Jesus reveals the Creator.

Evident at this point, a choice must be made; the reliability of the Bible must either be accepted or rejected. There can be no middle ground or conjecture here. C. S. Lewis, renowned Christian scholar and apologist of the twentieth century, is known for his summation of this point in his book *Mere Christianity*, when he states, "Christianity, if false, is of no importance, and if true, of infinite importance. The only thing it cannot be is moderately important." Without the Bible's development across 1400 years of ancient history, which includes the life of a historical Jesus as Christ and Messiah, no Christianity exists. I have settled this question for myself. The Bible is God-breathed, entirely true, and reveals the truth of the Lord God that we need to know.

Thereby, we find there is only one truth that orders the four conjectured levels into one. All truth is understood as *absolute* and therefore sourced from the Mind of the Eternal God. His thoughts and statements are the truth. By virtue of being an external standard, truth is unfettered by the corruptions of human feeling and limits of human thinking. The other three categories of universal, cultural, and individual are not truths at all. As constructs of thinking about being human by humans, affirmations of values and formations of propositions are all limited within the parameters established by mere humans. What we call truth not defined by absolute truth is the experiential composite known as *material reality* by humans. Any level of human experience either aligns with God's revelation of the truth, or the experience violates the truth. It looks like this:

Absolute Truth	**Truth–in and of God**	**Falsehood–outside of God**
Universal Experience	Core inner being aligned with and ordered by Divine Nature.	Unaligned with Divine Nature; Disordered inner being.
Cultural Experience	God's kingdom; foremost sense of group belonging; shared heritage and future under his authority.	Compounding errors of judgment conflict human association; corruption defines political/economic order.
Individual Experience	Individual develops and functions through submission to Holy Spirit.	Every individual is trapped by falsehoods outside of God's Presence.

The trustworthiness of biblical revelation of truth is of paramount importance. I would add two books that provide logical critical analysis and quantifiable evidence of the integrity of the Bible: *Cold-Case Christianity* by J. Warner Wallace. Mr. Wallace is a cold-case detective and applies the techniques and skill sets of that profession to examine the death and resurrection of Christ as recorded in the Bible. Second, pick up and read *Evidence that Demands a Verdict* by Josh McDowell and Sean McDowell, PhD. It is a carefully researched and documented testimony of the Bible's authenticity as what it claims to be, the Word of the God of Creation.

The Christian walk in the spirit of Jesus is a function of faith in absolute truth as detailed in the Bible. In the final analysis, the belief that Jesus is God on Earth and that the Bible accurately details a supernatural God interacting with humanity is a choice for seekers of truth to accept or reject.

Do not be confused by critics arguing that faith is unfounded and fruitless since the Bible or the God it reveals cannot be scientifically verified. Science places its faith in quantifiable data, but such data only answers questions about the material world. It takes faith to trust that the material world alone is the absolute truth for humanity. It takes faith to accept any construct of material knowledge as able to foster love and kindness or to provide controls for hate and cruelty. Faith is not a weakness; it is fundamental to igniting the drive of a forward-moving person. The issue is the source that one's faith draws upon. The material future is dim and unclear for every single human. We must decide what to trust to find strength and direction in this life, especially during this twenty-first century. To trust nothing leaves a human wallowing in despondency. To trust humanity is a misguided hope. To trust Jesus is the answer to all of our needs.

The qualitative data for trusting the Scriptures resounds in the stories of human beings—myself included—who testify to the reality of the Lord Jesus being alive and available today to those committed to him. I was reared in an alcoholic, broken home. As an adult, I pursued sinfulness deliberately, determined to fill my deepest needs. In that approach to life, I reaped only sorrow, damage to my body, and confusion in my thinking. Without meeting the Spirit of the living Jesus, there is no doubt I would have died unmarried and young. You would not be reading this book. The Scriptures are light from the heart of God. To read them, embrace them, and find the application described therein of living through his Holy Spirit is the transforming truth.

U is for the Ultimate Good Time
Universalism, Unity, Union

IN THE PREVIOUS CHAPTER, "The Transforming Truth," we examined levels of experiencing truth. Anyone's emotional capacities can alter the perception of reality, and the power of emotion will color perceived truth. This subjectivity in perceiving *truth* is a universal human experience, and a distinctive derivative of universal experiences, *universalism,* needs definition. It is the epitome of subjective thinking attempting to supply the spiritual needs of the heart.

As a theological term, universalism will be found in formal and general uses. The formal usage is humanistic and embraced by groups such as the Unitarian Universalist Organization. In this context, universalism means that all cultures have a version of God or other explanations for a moral structure defining right and wrong. Therefore, all religions are valid and equal. No one version of God is more significant than another, and everyone is on a path to an eternal heaven.

A second use of *universalism* is not associated with a particular group but is a theological position of some Christian-labeled teachers. In this context, universalism is labeled *universal salvation.* This proposition focuses on God's love as expansive and all-encompassing. Therefore, he will redeem everyone alive and all who have ever lived, opening eternal heaven to all souls who have traversed material creation. No one will face eternity separated from him.

Universalism, whether cross-cultural or labeled Christian, is a feel-good perspective. The cultural variant is a philosophical view on spiritual practice and human improvement. The formal usage of the term by Unitarian Universalists expresses an egalitarian acceptance that all voices on spiritual issues are equally valid. It is humanism with a purposeful mix of positivism and social activism. I submit it has no hope of changing the world for the better. In the second variation, the supposed *Christian* perspective, universal salvation is a belief system inconsistent with the Bible's whole counsel. It is conjecture moving into imaginative conclusions of the concept of God's love.

A logical reading of the Scriptures on salvation must conclude that the universalist acceptance of all spiritual explanations of deity and the idea of universal salvation within a Christian context both fail the hermeneutic process. Neither universal position adequately addresses the problem of the human condition of sin.

Multiple references to sin found in the New Testament include: all fornication, impurities of the heart and mind, sensuality, idolatry, sorcery, enmities, strife, jealousy, outbursts of anger, disputes, dissensions, envy, drunkenness, carousing, theft, swindling, reviling, being a lover of self, conceit, greed, arrogance, disobedience to parents, ungratefulness, unkindness, gossip, lack of self-control, brutality, betrayal, and love of pleasure. You get the idea, *sin* is the biblical term for the painful behaviors and attitudes that assail humanity. All these sins occur wherever people are on this swirling planet. I do not say this to throw stones at others. I participated in many behaviors on that list, and I still must maintain discipline against sinful impulses or ask forgiveness when I fail. There is neither condemnation nor hypocrisy in identifying the breadth of human states of being that harm people and poison society generally.

Universalism is a construct of thought springing from the Antichrist spirit. That is, both universalist acceptance of all deities and universal salvation necessarily involve rejecting the crucifixion and resurrection of Jesus. Neither position is in line with the Scriptures. Sinfulness blocks entrance into the Presence of God. God is love, but he is also holy justice as well.

The Bible predicts that in the end times, people will cry out for peace and safety (1 Thes 5:3).[1] These two desirable states are generally recognized as threatened by problems of violence, war, civil unrest, and unfair economic policies. Those wanting a better world espouse one solution for ushering humanity into an age of cooperation and mutual respect: eliminate divisiveness rooted in religious beliefs and related moral values. The identified human outcry for collective global peace and a safe social order drives the current clamor for unity among all humans.

---

1. Paraphrases adapted from the New American Standard Bible: ©2020 by the Lockman Foundation.

U is for the Ultimate Good Time

The bold presumption is that the humanity we know can see itself as spiritually united, and thus, each person behaves respectfully of all others. Could we humans educate ourselves into harmonious unity worldwide, where everyone behaves well toward everyone else? I think not. Examine the last two millennia historically. Is there any clue that the best intentions resulted in establishing a peaceful group able to model and lead the rest of the world into peaceful cooperation? Where is the data-supported historical development of any city-state, nation-state, or just a regional tribe of any size sharing borders with differing people groups in consistent cooperation? Peaceful cooperation occurs but is minimal in the records and fails as time passes.

What we observe across the history of civilization and what is happening around us now is unmitigated competition for resources and rivalry over wealth growth based on resource control. Whether we explain the competition as a function of natural selection in an evolutionary process or the effect of sin on God's creation, the material reality speaks for itself. Humans act inhumanely toward one another as individuals and in organized groups for various reasons, but the core issue is our selfishness and greed. The call for unity among all humans is an empty platitude.

The Bible teaches that the love of money, that is greed, is the root of all evil (1 Tim 6:10). Jesus came to redeem creation from a mire of violence rooted in greed and redirect the human heart to the God-intended state of love and peace. However, that process—labeled *sanctification*—is wholly dependent on a person dying to innate selfish desires. Refusal to follow intrinsic desires, a death to self, opens an individual to pursue the way of emotional stability and intellectual ordering of priorities true to God's divine nature.

Remember Jesus's words in John 14:6, "I am the way, the truth, and the life. No one comes to the Father but through me." Many Christians interpret this sentence as knowing Jesus is the only way to heaven.[2] Jesus alone

---

2. This verse is used as a prooftext that all who have not heard of Jesus cannot enter heaven. There is a difference between hearing of and then rejecting Christ contrasted with never having heard anything about him. The context of this Scripture is the instruction of Jesus, "Do not let your heart be troubled." Every statement following is the logic of trust in Jesus. We can trust Jesus to be fair and just while he sits on the great white throne of judgment. Those who hear and reject are sorted out from the hearers who accept. Why assume those who have never heard are damned? Yes, we should reach all we can with the gospel. What if those who have never heard of Jesus are judged by a different standard that is not stated anywhere? That standard being obedience to conscience, which was given by God in the beginning. Jesus judges and remains the door to the Father in such a

atones for our sins and being born of the spirit is our bridge into heaven (John 3:5). However, there is more meaning. Jesus modeled the way to be a human being. That is, by his Holy Spirit within our hearts, we are guided in the act of being human. The truth he reveals instructs the intellect in the moral understanding of reality, and the Holy Spirit delivers his very life force into our hearts. Walking in the spirit with Jesus is the ultimate good time on Earth.

Walking in the Spirit of God, we confront the constant logical task of being true to a vastly different set of motives and choices from the way of the world around us. The truth found only in God is politically and culturally rejected by the masses. We cannot help the world with its goal of unity. The world around us will never succeed in legislating a peaceful and just world system. As Christians, we have a dual purpose related to the political and cultural mess around us. First, we seek the Father, Son, and Holy Spirit to reflect his image and his ways to the world. Second, we announce that Christ will return and establish his government, his kingdom of truth, love, and justice on this Earth.

We are not enemies with other humans. However, we are enemies with the spiritual power that opposes God's truth and destroys people. The Scriptures teach us to remain openly among those who reject God, offering his love and his light, the truth to anyone who might listen. We travel our life's path and progress spiritually into the image of God intended at the creation, and speak the absolute truth amid an intellectually inconsistent and emotionally unstable world.

In contrast to the world seeking unity, Christians recognize and develop our union with God. Jesus taught that he and the Father are one. If we see him, we see the Father (John 14: 7–11). Jesus also prayed for us to be one with him and God the Father (John 17:16–21). This spiritual connection, stated in words, is the vibrant reality I want you to find. The spiritual life of Jesus residing in us as a gift of grace enables us to walk in the depth of love and truth from the heart of God the Father. The love shared by those following the Creator, teaches us how to love others. Love of God, in God, beckons as hope to all the burdened on earth.

The Father anointed Jesus for the spiritual work of defeating the pride and plans of Lucifer. Submission to the ways of the Holy Spirit is a choice

---

scenario. Mere supposition on my part? Yes. It is supposition based on Romans 2:12–16. I do not intend to refute traditional understanding of how salvation occurs. I am thinking outside the box. As in the dinosaurs, the Scriptures do not speak specific answers for every question we might frame.

we make. We are never bereft of our free will, and we lay ourselves at his feet because of the grace we received to new life by the atonement of Christ. By knowing the born-of-spirit experience, we gain the knowledge of an anointing on us, the Holy Spirit, who is the Spirit of the Anointed One, Jesus. We know union with God.

V is for Vessels of the Holy Spirit
Violence, Values, Virtue

DURING THE CUBAN MISSILE Crisis in 1962, our nation edged near the unimaginable peril of nuclear war. I remember well the school-wide drills we had in the event of a nuclear attack on the us. Students were to crawl beneath their desks into a fetal position, with arms covering the head. We also practiced speedy evacuation from the building. For the evacuation, the principal announced the drill near the end of school, and students were bussed or walked home. Since we left school fifteen minutes early, I was disappointed when the drills stopped. Living less than a mile from school, I walked. It crossed my mind that walking students would be especially vulnerable to any radiation, but I was glad to be dismissed early. In hindsight, I am confident that the Soviet Union never considered nuking our small town.

From Cain killing Abel to the daily violent crimes across U.S. society, humans spill each other's blood. Lethal violence by individuals, groups, and nations burdens our collective human experience with grief and fear. What causes all this violence? Sociological concerns focus on the statistical analysis of gender, race, and socioeconomic inequality.[1] A premeditated action or spontaneous passion resulting in murder reported by news media will often suggest possible motives. Inevitably, these motives are linked to human hatred, lust for power and sex, or desire for fame or wealth.

In the case of nations warring with one another, the justification for going to war is to answer the threat of the enemy and the subversion of the homeland's national values. In both the first and second world wars, a U.S. national value of defending democracy made the list of reasons for war. A similar observation can be made of the U.S. Civil War. North and South

---

1. Armstead, "Inequities in violence risks."

V is for Vessels of the Holy Spirit

held up their regionally developed differences as rooted in opposing value systems.

Values are an individual's identified principles for living. Choices concerning values are rooted in a teen's family upbringing and influences from society at large. The values adopted by anyone may or may not root in religious teachings. Atheists and theists will hold personal values, and may share some values. For example, the action of joining a community effort to clean up roadside litter reflects a value of environmental conservation; based on a shared value, both atheists and theists will work side by side due to a shared value.

Shared values among U.S. citizens underpin the political process. Political advocates appeal to constituent values, seeking support at the polls and resulting in the power to shape legislation. The two-party political system established in the U.S. Constitution is a mechanism for adjusting differences of opinion over values into laws governing all. In contrast, many democracies use a parliamentary or multi-party system, but the dynamic of values joining people together for voting power exists within democracies worldwide. Values prioritize an individual's decision-making as an individual and as a member of a voting block.

The important principles guiding anyone's decision-making usually adds *morals* and *ethics* to values. Morals are principles governing human behavior known and understood through religious instruction. Morals state clear standards of right and wrong applicable to sexual intimacy and issues of justice. It understandably follows that shared morals create a bond of commitment to common goals among those who believe in the presumed supernatural source.

Ethics derive their basis and application within a social institution or professional setting. The practice of law, medicine, education, or business all maintain ethical standards for their respective fields; thus, entering a profession means adopting and working with fidelity to an identified ethics code. Ethics foster community among colleagues but typically do not establish the commitment bonding of shared religious affiliation.

Divisive issues in the United States often gain their nature and intensity as matters of disagreement concerning the Constitution. An example is the national debate over gun ownership versus gun restrictions. Specifically, the cultural divide pits gun ownership rights against the high rate of murder by firearms. Gun owners believe gun violence against humans is a mental health issue, and restrictions on gun ownership does not justly address the problem of violence. The voice of the opposing side calls for stricter regulation of gun sales to alleviate the harm and heartache of gun deaths. These folks demand protection of the safety and welfare of the population generally.

Political advocacy for both positions builds from a construct of values. Gun owners list values of self-protection, protection of family or property, and the maintenance of rights granted by the "Bill of Rights." Gun control advocates stand on the values of protecting individuals, establishing a more peaceful social order, and relief from associated fear and suffering. The argument between the two groups reduces to whose values the government will reflect in establishing the laws we all must live by.

A tiny percentage of any population inflicts the violence of murder, but every human experiences feelings of vengeance. When confronted by false, unjustified accusations, or worse, any violent actions intent on harm, an ordinary human reaction is a vengeful desire to target the source of the attack. Unleashed vengeance within any individual can result in misconstrued conclusions and dangerous, impulsive actions. Vengeance acted upon erupts from an inward spiritually driven path. Vengeful feelings are a common emotional reaction for most humans. In some people, vengeance broods and morphs into imagined actions of retribution. The acceptance of harmful action against the emotional or physical well-being of a person objectified by vengeance as a deserving target is a road map to violence.

In the last chapter, we examined the union with God. Christianity fails in authenticity if practiced as a moral code only. Authentic Christianity is a state begun by accepting that Christ has revoked the power of spiritual death. Maturation of the spiritual state of being in Christ occurs over time, steadily increasing the believer's self-awareness of motivations. The believer learns to hear and trust the Holy Spirit in choosing virtuous emotions over natural but negative emotional force.

How do emotional perceptions and choices occur in the spirit? How do we learn to reject reactions such as vengeance and thus avoid harmful actions against others? The insight and strength needed must spring from the understanding of being one with God. Humility, chosen through trust in the Holy Spirit within the heart, guides evaluative thinking which rejects negative emotions and seeks instead to effect action aligned with God's love and holiness.

An active seeking of the guidance of the Holy Spirit is informed intellectually by God's Word and actively used in faith. The practice of rejecting one's negative emotions is a learned skill. Becoming more skillful at spirit-led governance of the emotions is often pursued after compulsive reactions have hurt others. Do not consider failure to control such reactions as evidence that you are not a Christian. Eruption of sinful attitudes or actions is evidence you need more maturity. More humility and seeking to know a deeper love of God is the path forward.

Vengeance rooted in the presumption that another person is deserving of punishment is one of many false conditional motives that attempt to hold power over us after being born again in spirit. The new creature reckons the negative impulses as harmful and learns by trial and error how to preempt impulsiveness and seek instead wholesome, virtue-oriented responses. We do not choose morality because we are committed to morality; we choose to abide in him, and he is moral and just—wholly and essentially.

The biblical basis for describing the union with God as a practical material earth experience is not a point-by-point description in any given chapter. Instead, we collect a preponderance of scriptural evidence working together. Two foundational examples are John 15:5–9 and 17:20–23. Memorizing and mentally reciting these two excerpts as a routine part of one's stream of consciousness strengthens the heart.

Further in regard to practical in-the-spirit reckoning, Hebrews 4:12 supplies the starting point for understanding the quest for the believer's spirit-union identity with the Holy Spirit. The verse reads, "For the word of God is alive and active. Sharper than any double-edged sword, it penetrates even to dividing soul and spirit, joints and marrow; it judges the thoughts and attitudes of the heart."

The phrase identifying a division between soul and spirit is followed by a literary parallelism. The metaphor "of bone and marrow" in the verse likens a soul to a structural bone and the spirit to a life-sustaining substance. The two terms, *soul* and *spirit* are part of the immaterial realm but are reckoned in this verse as distinct from each other.

Three vital aspects of the soul determine destiny on earth: desire, will, and conscience. None of these are taught or given by anyone to anyone. These three attributes of the soul intertwine as a guidance and propulsion system embedded within human consciousness. The conscience and the will aim the guidance system, while desire propels action. Desire stirs from either of two generating sources: the Spirit of Jesus Christ or the spirit of the Antichrist.

Regeneration in Jesus 101

The human spirit is a complex matrix of related intellectual constructs, emotional states, values, attitudes, individual goals, and reactions to the outer world. The One, the Spirit above, is truth, love, and the Master of Creation. The other is a smoke-and-mirrors counterfeit, claiming satisfaction results through inflated pride, holding to unreasonable fear, and seduction to sensual pleasures.

Our education system focuses on developing the intellect, but a human also needs awareness of the structures and functions of the inner being: heart, soul, and the directional wind of spirit. No one has seen a soul under a microscope or by any other earthly means. The harsh reality of the human condition is that we are born with a broken guidance system. The conscience and will are in place, but the desire in every born soul is tuned to seek the satisfaction of self. In Jesus, our emotional needs are fulfilled, and desires are ordered toward virtue. We process life experiences differently and learn how to relinquish fear, pride, and self-interest rather than be ruled by them. The indwelling Holy Spirit guides us in the use of replacement strategies: identifying all choices functioning in the matrix of the old nature's selfishness and refusing to act on them; then focusing the eyes of the heart on our understanding of truth and love through Jesus's teaching and sacrifice, we act in that understanding. Our priorities change.

The written Word contains over three hundred uses of the term *spirit* in the New Testament and over two hundred occurrences in the Old Testament.[2] Those who hear and understand that Jesus was the life and that his life lights the way for humanity will receive God's plan to deliver humanity from the grip of God's enemy, Lucifer (John 1:4).[3]

Accepting Jesus Christ as Savior and seeking to walk in the spirit found through his Holy Spirit is to walk a new path in life. Going down this path does not make any person perfect. The path is fraught with misjudgments, wrong choices, and failure to understand. The first and overarching change is simple but eternally profound; the new believer gains an actual choice between good and evil for the first time. In understanding the union with God, we accept the biblical metaphor that we are a cup, a vessel, into which has been poured the living water, the Holy Spirit.

As vessels of the Holy Spirit, we reject presumptions about life's meaning stemming from subjective desire and self-interest, and replace all false

---

2. Zondervan, *spirit*, 1054–1056.

3. Paraphrases adapted from the New American Standard Bible: ©2020 by the Lockman Foundation.

V is for Vessels of the Holy Spirit

cultural constructs with the insight and power of compassion found in God's goodness. Spiritually full of the Holy Spirit, humans are no longer merely animals striving to survive in a jungle. We are sons and daughters of the Eternal God, living as subjects in his kingdom of righteousness. Within this hurting world, we live as vessels of peace and virtue.

W is for Wrestling with God
Wandering, Why, Wisdom

OKAY, I KNOW IT is evident; I am a boomer. Many of my age were involved in the Christian church growing up, but my parents did not lead our family into church life nor teach my siblings and me about the Lord Jesus. As a freshman in high school, I started attending a Methodist church on my own. My parents had divorced, my mom remarried, and I plopped down in a new school system. Going to church struck me as a way to make new friends, which worked. My mom and stepdad were uninterested in attending but willing to take me back and forth for church services and youth group activities. My exposure to the power of the Bible began.

I attended a church-sponsored summer camp between my sophomore and junior years of high school. Near the end of that week, I committed to Christ, and I must report that we did sing "Kum Ba Yah!" Today, that phrase is frequently a mocking allusion to religious sentimentality. Those three words are a request that God draw near and relieve human suffering.

Beloved teen, gathered within these pages are thoughts and insights not provided to me as adulthood loomed ahead. The functioning institutional church stirred hope in me that wisdom and understanding rested within the space illuminated through the stained glass. Yet, the rituals, pulpit-spoken instructions, and exhortations did not open the eyes of my heart to the reality of walking with God. I finished high school wearing a cross around my neck for all to see, but my inner sinful desire lived on, demanding freedom for self-fulfillment as defined by me.

Following high school, I won a scholarship to a private Christian college in North Georgia. My faith wilted in a core-required religion course. The scrutiny generated by the syllabus offered a comparative analysis of Christianity, Judaism, Islam, and Buddhism. The singularity and power of

Jesus as the One to be worshiped fell away; in its place evolved the conclusion that keeping the Golden Rule was all a human owed as a response to a god who might be out there.

I reckoned my sinful desires as not sinful after all. I walked away from the crucified and resurrected Christ as the only way to know God. My life degenerated into profligate patterns. I wandered, tethered to self-indulgence, for four and a half years. I never stayed anywhere longer than six months while I crossed the continental United States four times and traversed the East Coast states from New York to Florida more than a dozen times. A conclusion I had justified as freedom from a perceived chain of moral conformity wrecked my mental health and threatened my physical well-being.

I am not a man of any outstanding achievements who wields significant influence in this world. I speak from personal experience and study. I strive in these words to shine a light on the Truth in the Bible and invite your serious thought and determination toward a deeper walk with God. At the very least, I seek your recognition of a difference between experiencing God as Father, Son, and Holy Spirit versus the status of a churchgoer. I hope you will find confident assurance that the Bible reveals three realities: our Father God's everlasting love and holiness; his Son Jesus as our King and Savior; and the Holy Spirit, God with us, given to comfort and guide us.

The Truth written in the Bible cries out for all humanity to hear. The Truth includes the Father's invitation to receive the flow of an unparalleled supply for one's inner being called the living water by Jesus. The living water refreshes the soul, enlightens the mind, and strengthens the heart of anyone accepting the atonement of Christ and the rebirth of spirit (John 4:10).[1] The life of the Holy Spirit within is the living water and links directly with the *river of life* recorded in Revelation 22:1.

If the Bible is true, why are Christians sometimes such a poor reflection of God? Are we all just hypocrites? *Christian* is a self-identified moniker, and people claiming it may behave according to motivations misaligned with God's written intentions. Examples include:

- delusional (disconnect from reality and not hypocritical),
- well intentioned folks misinformed by humanist thinking,
- wolves in sheep's clothing (intentional hypocrisy),

---

1. Paraphrases adapted from the New American Standard Bible: ©2020 by the Lockman Foundation.

- individuals or whole churches walking in apostasy,
- informed by biblical truth but not understanding the application thereof (seed falling on rocky ground: Matt 13:20–21),
- understanding many applications but immature in living by the Holy Spirit (seed choked by thorns: Matt 13:22).

Overall, people often state their belief in Jesus as God, but they lack spiritual maturity. Immaturity is not hypocrisy. Maturing in spirit occurs through a lifetime of experiences. It is not like taking a class and passing an end-of-term exam. People receive salvation through the atonement, then live while learning the ways of spirit life. We might state that as learning the way of holiness or of being filled by God.

An additional roadblock to maturity is something called *conventional wisdom*. Conventional wisdom develops over time as a population of people generally adopts a particular response to a life circumstance as logical and practical. Conventional wisdom is frequently synonymous with points of view labeled *common sense*. If we form our opinions based on the weight of conventional wisdom or its cousin, common sense, we may find ourselves aligned with others but at odds with God.

The Christian's goal is to live as a supplicant and press into spiritual maturity. A mature spirit means that through God's Presence within, one exhibits a disciplined will (the power to choose), grounded in love for God and others. When our motivations align with this cornerstone of Christianity, the faithful exercise of one's will in the ways of God speaks with clarity to the reality of the biblical revelation. Thus, we conclude from Romans 8:19, ". . . the anxious longing of the creation waits eagerly for the revealing of the sons of God," is satiated. Here is a beautiful spiritual fact: faith in God results in sound judgment within the believer (Rom 12:3). That last statement also describes what wisdom looks like: stabilizing faith making personal judgments strong and sound.

Dying to self as submission to God is the Christian experience that begins at water baptism. Then real life follows, and our commitment faces many tests. Life brings pain: the death of loved ones, enemies who desire to exploit or humiliate, personal moral failure, and others. Challenges from outside us stir questions within, which we must confront as an opportunity to deepen our spiritual understanding and fuel our spiritual growth. In working through complex circumstances of pain, we often confront difficult questions. We either turn from God or turn to him.

W is for Wrestling with God

A bulwark of intertwined comfort, strength, and guidance forms as the searching Christian interacts with the Bible and the Presence of the Holy Spirit within. In the crucible of emotional pain, we learn the ways and means of the Holy Spirit. Walk with God, and he will lead through all situations. Engagement with God amid pain and the choosing of obedience will result in wisdom gained. Strength, peace, and insight stem from wisdom and position one for growth in more wisdom. Though the cost of discipleship is high, depth in the Lord is a blessing beyond anything we conceive or request.

A curious story in Genesis is of Jacob wrestling with God. (Some commentators call the man wrestling with Jacob an angel, but in Genesis 32:30 Jacob states after the event, "I have seen God face to face.") Jacob struggles mightily with this physical manifestation of God. Near morning and the end of the match, Jacob states he will not stop until he receives a blessing. God touches Jacob's hip, and he leaves the event walking with a limp. God blesses him and renames Jacob, Israel, but the encounter marks him for life.

God intends to bless us with the glory of being in him. People tend to define blessings in material terms, but the spiritual insight we gain by learning to abide in Christ is a blessing that is never exhausted. Moving into the spiritual blessings of abundant life requires a continuing decrease of one's limited, selfish thoughts supplanted with increasing thoughts inspired while abiding in God.

Jacob wrestled with God, perhaps unaware with whom; but in realizing the identity of the being, Jacob sought to turn the struggle into receiving a blessing. It is important that we do not consider resisting the way of God or other selfish decisions causing painful circumstances as a "wrestling with God" experience. Jacob's experience illustrates what it means to persist in prayer for God's spiritual touch.

The consequence of wrestling with our Father for his blessing alters us to greater dependence on him. The outcome of pursuit of the Father's will in blessing may simply be an increase in understanding one's dependence on him. Remember Jesus instructing the disciples about child-like dependence on God (Matt 18:2–3)?

A believer might categorize individual prayer as wrestling with God for many good reasons. Like many spiritual issues, if we seek answers or understanding from our personal experience and knowledge, we will be limited by our inductive approach to comprehension. Instead, wisdom seeks answers in and through the Holy Spirit available to us. We must see ourselves in the big picture of God's purposes and deduce our responses from his outside vantage point. Three key principles of wisdom:

- wisdom begins with reverence for the LORD (Prov 9:10).
- choices according to love are always wise and yield understanding (1 Cor 13).
- blindness to truth labels wisdom as foolishness or worse (1 Cor 2:6–16).

In baptism, we take the first step of dying to self. In walking with God, we accept life as the lessons needed for spirit maturation. Growth in spirit will mean that we tackle head-on into what we know and don't know about God. This state seeks a deeper knowledge and experience of his love. We are not wrestling with whether or not we believe in Jesus as God; we wrestle for a deeper understanding of him. It is wrestling with God to gain the blessing of his hand and heart. When the dust settles, we are more inclined to submit to spiritual disciplines.

In disciplining ourselves in the ways of the Lord, that is the abundant spirit-life he intends for us, wisdom from God and in God results. The practice of wisdom builds the kingdom of God in our hearts, complete with its righteousness, peace, and joy. Thus, wisdom governs our actions, and we as mere humans live and reveal the Father, Son, and the Holy Spirit.

X is for Christ, as in Xmas
Xenophobia, eXistentism, eXalted

IN SCHOOL DURING THE 1960s, a red X over any punctuation mark, word, number, or even a whole paragraph starkly indicated a wrong answer. Lots of them jumping off the front page of a test, justifying the grade at the top, caused slunking shoulders. The lack of them meant smiling self-congratulation. Right and wrong answers still matter on paper-based exams, but as a way to communicate, "Dear Student, your answer is a miss," the red X has lost favor. Change in educational procedures does not surprise anyone, but X still marks the spot of the buried treasure on any pirate's map. What is right or wrong behavior matters, but changing values and resulting rancor rip at the social fabric within U.S. culture.

Consider *xenophobia*, the fear of and hatred for anything strange or foreign, particularly people from other countries.[1] Human relations, as well as international interactions, are negatively impacted by xenophobia. Historically, many recorded events are energized in part or in whole by fear and hatred of people from foreign regions. Wars have complicated roots, but xenophobia is often a cause or an exacerbating factor. From tribal wars in primitive cultures through today's conflicts between Russians/Ukrainians and Palestinians/Jews, hatred abounds and is focused against the people across the boundary line.

A xenophobic attitude and action may also drive a country's foreign policy in an opposite direction. Your high school's world history may have included the Ming Dynasty of China, which ruled from the 14th to the 17th centuries. If so, you are already aware that following many years of significant exploration by sea, the Ming Dynasty decided all cultures beyond China to be inferior. A Chinese isolationist foreign policy lasting for

1. Merriam Webster's, *xenophobia*, 1369.

centuries resulted. Instead of aggression due to xenophobia, China withdrew from involvement with nations. Xenophobia, like other fears, stems from the natural human outlook of self-preservation.

The opposite of xenophobia, patriotism impacts our national cohesion. Blocks of voters consider patriotism, an intense loyalty to one's country and pride in a heritage of shared national values, as vitally important to the United States. Patriotism as an individual construct, when multiplied across a national population becomes a wave of sentiment powering political advocacy. The comparative societal forces of xenophobia and patriotism build from two primary identified factors of human emotion: fear and pride. Fear is the motivating force behind xenophobia, just as pride is the driving factor in patriotism. Both xenophobia and patriotism exemplify non-material terms for facets of spirit realm stuff influencing groups of people.

Xenophobia and patriotism represent ideas with significant emotional depth for large numbers of people. People identifying in solidarity over the sentiments underlying these representative terms may form an unorganized social force calling for action. Groups with a shared goal for social action or change form a *movement*. Movements develop ad hoc, but quickly cause more formalized groups to form. Organization brings money and other resources together to help build the movement to a wider acceptance across a society.

Within the concept of a movement, we find a historical, recurring spiritual force: human desire for freedom of self-determination will drive social change. Specific examples of such movements in the United States include:

- British colonists of the eighteenth century stirring rebellion against monarchical power.

- Abolitionists of the nineteenth century challenging the economic institution of slavery.

- The youth of the mid twentieth century questioning and rebelling against existing political, economic, and social institutions.

However, social change does not rely solely on emotionally charged movements.

Philosophy seeks logic and wisdom to describe three overarching strands of culture: reality, truth, and beauty. It's a broad topic. Philosophy as a discipline does not have the goal of social change. However, proposed philosophic perspectives concerning individuals and society help connect like-minded people looking for ways to explain the social world.

The list of famous philosophers spans the globe and the last two millennia: Confucius, Kant, Lao Tzu, Locke, Marx, Nietzsche, Voltaire, among many others. Associated with philosophers are named philosophies. Stoicism, Epicureanism, Nihilism, Marxism, and Hedonism are a few that come to mind.

Existentialism is a philosophical position that addresses human existence in the context of universal truths. Existentialism is a relatively recent addition to the arena of philosophical analyses. Existentialism is "a philosophical movement embracing diverse doctrines but centering on analysis of individual existence in an unfathomable universe and the plight of the individual who must assume ultimate responsibility for acts of free will without any certain knowledge of what is right or wrong or good or bad."[2]

Existentialism identifies the human experience as a negative condition. The term *plight*, "an unfortunate, difficult, precarious situation" indicates that perception.[3] U.S. citizens face major consequences in the midst of available choices, and the variations of cultural standards for right or wrong and good or bad spur high levels of anxiety for many of us. Anxiety erupting over the meaning of one's existence carries a label in psychological jargon: *existential angst*.

Existentialism as a philosophical construct reaches its conclusion within the glare of human understanding predicated on atheism—"unfathomable universe" and "no certain knowledge of right or wrong"—then presumes to call the human experience a *plight* of circumstances. It is victimization language explaining what it feels like living in a cold, random, amoral world. In existentialism and other philosophical positions, the rationalizations espoused are developed inductively from experiences occurring in and as a function of the state of humanity. A humanity separated from God. Consequently, logic with no connection to the well of the heart produces conclusions missing the meaning and purpose of God and his Word.

As compelling as any world philosophy, experiential group alignment, social movement, or revered tradition may appear, these cannot connect a human being with the divine nature of the Creator God. Without the spiritual connection prescribed by our Lord God and Father, the acceptance of Jesus Christ for deliverance from innate human selfishness, none receives

---

2. Merriam Webster's, *existentialism*, 407.
3. Merriam Webster's, *existentialism*, 407.

the Holy Spirit. Thus, without being born of the spirit through God's grace, a human being lives looking for answers with angst or choosing lesser states as fulfilling spiritual needs and potential.

The death of spirit that the Lord warned would come to Adam and Eve—a warning that the enemy of God falsely claimed was not valid—remains to this day in every human heart (Gen 2:17; 3:2–3).[4] As such, the meaning and purposes of God and his Word cannot be discerned due to a dead spirit and living physically in the glare of selfishness. People who do not know the Lord Jesus live in varied states of understanding their material experience. Look around, read through the historical record, and among the stories of glory and success find a manifestation of shifting standards driving the political, religious, and economic power spheres.

As we near the wrap-up of this book, an X represents the first letter of the word *Christ* as rendered in Greek, which means *anointed*.[5] Jesus Christ is the source of life on Earth, according to the Apostle John (John 1:2). He is the promised Messiah of the Jews (John 4:25–26). He is the Savior of *anyone* who believes in him and receives forgiveness (Acts 10:43). His appearance on Earth and the revelations he spoke are the primary markers of the absolute substance of living the regenerated Christian life.

The varied topics rendered in these pages are but a glimpse of the profound and singular experience of walking in the Spirit of the Lord Jesus. He is the marked spot of the treasure; he is the Pearl (Matt 13:46). The person born of the Spirit of God exalts Jesus above all (Eph 1:22). The Christian walk of faith is achieved by the filling of the inner being from Jesus Christ's spirit-life pouring like water into the believer as the Holy Spirit (John 4:14).

Our faith must extend beyond belief in the crucifixion and resurrection of Jesus. Those two events are the foundation on which stands faith in the promise of a continuing communion with the Lord God through the Holy Spirit. Jesus supplies the well of the heart with the gift of the Holy Spirit. Faith in the whole message of the gospel is a state of being fully human and living in the light of a truth-and-love boundary. The foundation is the miracle of being born a second time and the boundary is the continuing renewal based on the image of the One who created us (Col 3:10).

The vital key for spiritual understanding is two-fold: an applied reasoning over the written Word and the embrace of the will in obedience to an

---

4. Paraphrases adapted from the New American Standard Bible: ©2020 by the Lockman Foundation.

5. McEvoy, "Christos Meaning."

active Presence of God within our being. He lifts our vision to the vantage point of evaluation outside of our limited subjectivity, as mentioned previously. We must compare ourselves to a trusted standard not defined by mere human understanding, such as existentialism or patriotism and all wholly human constructs inductively established within limited human weakness.

We adopt a perspective that transcends human limitations. To grow emotionally as the new creature in the spirit of Jesus, we study the Bible, accept it as the revelation of absolute truth, and apply its teachings to our thoughts, emotions, actions. The standard for morality is not a set of rules, but rather a Person. As Christians, we understand ourselves and others deductively from the premise that the Bible is the truth. Anything less than a response to the Spirit-revealed transformation of being is not Christianity.

A miracle is any expression of the supernatural acting on the natural. The Scripture states that the creation itself reveals God to us (Rom 1:20). The earth, this combine of atmosphere-lithosphere-hydrosphere, is a miracle. The celestial sphere stuns; the sparkle of a 100 billion suns pierces the cold, black-inked space and is a miracle. Dressed by daylight, the vision of stars strewn across that dark canopy vanishes behind another metaphor of God, that azure sky—a counterpoint of miracles. As an astronomical construct, the Earth, precisely distanced from the sun energizing every biome and sustaining all life forms therein is a miracle. The human body alive on that precisely placed planet is a container for one soul—miraculous. The revelation of the Bible, describing, explaining, and informing our human awareness of the nature of the soul and spirit, is a miracle.

Jesus Christ is central to both Creation and God's plan to reclaim humanity from his enemy, Lucifer, the source of all falsehood. Jesus is exalted above all other human beings. Jesus is the revealed power of God and the instruction for living in the spirit; he is the treasure of knowledge and wisdom (Col 2:3).

Y is for Your Life is Hidden
Youth, Yowl, Yield

THE MAN STANDING BEHIND me wore a mask, most likely a leftover decision from the Covid 19 scare. The wrinkles and gray hair placed him age-wise near my own grayed-head years. He and I were customers needing propane in the aftermath of the wallop Hurricane Helene dumped on our North Carolina mountain home. We exchanged names and compared stories of life without power for a second week.

As folks do, we commented on our nation and the upcoming presidential election. Not knowing each other's political leanings, our initial foray into that topic was cautious and polite. Next, Mr. Moretz surprised me by bringing up religion.

He opined, "If God is not mad at the us, he ought to be!" With that pop of a starting gun, we were off like a pair of runners, sharing views shaped by our combined decades of Christian life. Only a few statements later, he lamented, "I try so hard to keep all the rules, but I just can't seem to do it."

This brief exchange illustrates that Christianity varies from group to group. Some variations reduce the gospel to conformity with the presumed correct behavior of the group. Ironically, pulpit precepts intended to honor God's holiness can guide an entire family of believers onto a path of rules with most wearing a guilty-conscience backpack for failure. Spirit-life in the Lord transcends the misinformation within the extremes of sectarian legalism and universalist or libertine formulas.

We easily find within the ancient biblical text the relevant, expansive insight of knowing the Spirit of Jesus. The biblical story of a created humanity deluded by an enemy, that is delivered from falsehood by Jesus unfolds with the first reading. Within that overarching story is rich scriptural detail regarding how any human may gain fulfillment through the indwelling Presence of the Holy Spirit.

Teens manifest self-awareness, envisioning their future autonomy and power of choice. Influenced by an individual's nature-nurture experience, the parameters of the imagined adult life evoke a wide range of emotions. Youth becoming people free of fear and strong decision-makers are goals of conscientious parents. However, the Bible goes further and describes the redeemed human as capable of achieving spiritual maturity. Those old words reveal how anyone may join with God and thereby express God's love from the heart. As well, a transformed mind learns sound decision-making guided by faith in God's standards (Rom 12:2–3).[1]

This alphabetical trek, *Regeneration in Jesus 101*, contrasts the natural person and the spirit-regenerated Christian. The following table, "The Basic Human," organizes the subtopics discussed herein based on Jesus' instruction to love the Lord with one's whole being: heart, soul, mind, and strength (Mark 20:30–31).

The Basic Human	Heart	Soul	Mind	Strength
Characteristics	pride, fear, love, hate	will, desire, conscience	cognition, imagination	physicality, sensuality
Psychological Needs	attachment	self-enhancement	order and structure	pleasure, pain avoidance
Basic Life Questions	What is beauty?	Why am I here?	What is truth?	What is real?
Societal Organizers	power of symbols	arts, sciences, sports	institutions, law, traditions	productivity, resources conflict
US Cultural Forces	religion	media, technology	representative government	capitalism
Biblical Sin Categories	lust of the eyes	selfish nature; me emphasis	pride of life	lust of the flesh
Fallen Nature Identity	self-image idolatry	self-willed, natural desire	inductively based logic	my body, my expression
Regenerated Identity	humility, worship of God, union with God	will/desire align with God, clean conscience	deductively built on truth revealed by Jesus	temple of the Holy Spirit, God's hands and feet

---

1. Paraphrases adapted from the New American Standard Bible: ©2020 by the Lockman Foundation.

Note: The organization of topics presented is an overview of human complexity and interactions with culture, nothing more. For example, "science" listed under "soul" represents an outcome of the will and desire to know more about physical reality. No definitive conclusion should be drawn from "science" not being listed in the "mind" column.

In the midst of expectations and dreams for the adult life ahead of you, remember U.S. culture grapples with a multitude of issues to yowl over. Conflicting versions of human events recounted in news reports or classroom lectures produce negative assertions and shrill reactions. Social media threads evidence sharp disagreements over the examined narratives and a raucous anger across our society. Divisive issues include wealth distribution, climate change, politics, justice, racism, sexism, bigotry, transgender identity, and more.

As Christians, our primary concern should be our relationship with God. When knowing him orders our perspective on being human, we recognize both the calamities of a sinful society and the clamoring for justice as a mess that Lucifer purposely incites, and which God will ultimately redress. Does that mean we sit by and do nothing? No, of course not. The point is, we order ourselves in God, then approach the issues around us, in contrast with becoming dominated by humanistic observations and goals, then determining a skewed view of God based on a logic formed within the human condition. Such inductively contrived understanding is the basis of world religions, including a significant number of those labeled as Christian.

The unique objective of Christian faith is knowing God as the Author of life and as the continual source of the life known as in the spirit. It directly follows that four categories of people exist relative to him:

- those reared as believers in God as revealed to humanity by Jesus Christ;
- those reared believing there is no God, and therefore Jesus is not God;
- those who hold to other idealized forms of deity instead of the triune God of the Bible;
- those who have never heard of Jesus or the Bible.

All but the last enter adulthood either accepting or rejecting the Bible as the information that guides all exercise of will and desire.

Serious consideration of Christian faith discovers far more than an assured ticket into a heavenly afterlife. Faith in the one, true God is more than a Western Civilization theological assessment rooted in an ancient, 1400 years-long compilation of writings named the Holy Bible.

Authentic faith is an in-the-spirit condition which begins with **Who**, the non-material reality of God. Reading the Bible, we center on Jesus as God revealed in human form. Jesus promised the Holy Spirit would be given to his followers, and if professing Jesus as Lord, we need to identify, quantify, and qualify the why, how, when, and where one lives in the spirit by his Holy Spirit.

Why we dedicate ourselves to following Jesus is the trustworthiness of God. The spirit-life stands on one basic faith principle: God's character. The Bible reveals he is trustworthy through the Father giving his Son to satisfy the judgment against human sinfulness, and his Son accepting his own sacrifice for us. Further, God's character is seen throughout the profound beauty and power of his directive instructions on being human and living as God's image. Additionally, his character is affirmed in the testimonies from multitudes of people since Jesus walked on earth. The final evidence that God is trustworthy is the antithetical manifestation, the ubiquitous inhumanity of all hate, greed, and lust precipitated by the god of this world, Lucifer. That evil is so obvious drives a final *why*, the biblical imperative to live the good that overcomes all evil (Rom 12:21).

How we walk in spiritual life is based on a twofold application of truth: accepting God's love and loving him back in return. Spirit life is first and foremost relational. Seeking personal sanctification is the process of seeking the life of Christ within us (Col 3:1–3). We purpose to learn the way of love as patient, kind, and more (1 Cor 13:4–6). We manifest the right way in matters of justice, the practice of mercy, and choosing humility before God (Mic 6:8). Spirit-life results from a disciplined search for and learning from the state of union with God.

When and **where** are all-encompassing—always and in all circumstances. We continually persevere, the when, in aligning with the will of God as directed in the Bible (Jas 1:4). The spirit-life in Christ begins in the here and now. Here are seven practical suggestions for understanding spirit-life, the walk with God:

1. Avoid imagining that God speaks directly to you in the stream of consciousness. Accept all thoughts as your own. Wondering *if* God has directly spoken within one's thoughts creates confusion and easily fosters errors in judgment. Instead, purpose to learn truth from Scripture and filter one's thoughts accordingly. Learn to make decisions about what to

accept and what to reject of all thoughts. Filtering, accepting, and rejecting thoughts relies on one's conscience. This filtering is a mental discipline that manages the stream of consciousness, grows the understanding of spiritual information, and reaps an insight into the ways of the Lord.

Am I saying a believer never hears any thought directly from God? No. I am not trying to describe how God chooses to manifest himself to any believer. I am speaking about how any believer initially learns to handle the receiving end of his inspiration.

Paul's instruction is to think on whatever is true, honorable, right, pure, lovely, of good report, virtuous, and worthy of praise (Phil 4:8). This aligns with his imperative to pray without ceasing (1 Thes 5:17).

Managing one's constant flow of thoughts as a prayer is a cognitive function of the union with the Holy Spirit in the heart. Over time, as we faithfully develop our mental focus on the things above, God will judge the readiness of each follower and teach hearing from him in varied ways. As the Author and Perfecter of our faith, he will accomplish an ever-deepening understanding of hearing from him.

2. In addition to our thoughts, we must filter and manage our feelings. Feelings develop from an array of nature/nurture factors. Often, a person cannot fully ascertain why or from where a feeling comes. Conversely, an individual will experience a feeling and determine exactly the source and reason for a feeling.

Like one's thoughts, feelings are individual. The emotional states we generalize as feelings are subject to change and function in a moment. Likewise, these states may occur over time, limiting us rather than being managed by us. In this circumstance, an individual may identify any amorphous feeling as definitive of personal reality, a syndrome of being self-ruled by conclusions based on emotional experience. A relevant example is the situation lately termed *gender dysphoria*. People will feel something repeatedly and falsely determine it is the essence of their being. (I speak from personal experience on this topic. There is no hate in calling a set of specific feelings, false.)

Feelings are a bit like a tea kettle, ready to steam up if heat is applied. There are reasons for one's feelings, but the interpretation of what feelings represent is subjective and prone to misunderstanding. One's response to feelings is a choice. Our willingness to accept feelings as truth to be served is the platform for confusion, or worse, delusion.

Based on whether we are in the flesh or the spirit, we either succumb to personal desires or we manifest obedience above our natural desires. If we have embraced spirit life from God, we will be equipped for positive growth in the management of feelings. He holds our inner being and opens the understanding of one's circumstances, which provides insight into what our feelings represent.

Learning the rest in God, and taking time to do so in the prayer closet is the source of filtering and managing one's feelings. Think of it as learning the depths of the wellspring of the heart (Prov 4:23). The biblical directive over the hearing of God is simple, "Be still." Those two words indicate choosing governance of feelings to enter a sincere, at-rest state before God, a living Presence within us (Ps 4:4; Isa 30:18–21). This act of listening for God in our hearts sounds poetic, but it is practical and needed for growing more mature in spirit.

The experience of listening to the still, small voice of God is the initiative on our part to listen within both the mind and emotions for the Holy Spirit's guidance. In a moment of reflection, meditation, or prayer, the believer finds inspiration, inclination, and insight from God. It might be called the *whisper of the Holy Spirit*. The believer experiences an anointed moment that leads to an exercise of the will toward holiness, love, or both.

A word of caution: nothing we attribute to hearing God while in stillness will ever violate Scripture. As anyone grows in spiritual listening, there are other ways God may speak. These practical tips are offered as a starting point for learning God's voice. What develops between a believer and the Lord over time will likely go beyond the suggestions shared here.

3. Recognize when you are *not* in the spirit. If the fruit of the Spirit is love, joy, peace, patience, kindness, goodness, faithfulness, gentleness, and self-control, then any opposite actions or words are evidence of not walking in the new heart. This is the ongoing struggle between the flesh and the spirit (John 3:6; Rom 8:5). Are you being unloving, distressed, anxious, impatient, unkind, ungodly, unfaithful, harsh, or out of control? None of this second list flows from God. It all originates from the natural person. Stop in any of these moments and refocus on him.

Learning to be still during quiet prayer or meditation in the midst of daily challenges is a learned spiritual maturity. What God gives in the quiet time, teaches us how to hold our hearts amid the circumstances and demands of the day. It is the yielded, at-rest heart that is able to express the fruit of the Holy Spirit (Gal 5:16, 22–23). Paul understood such mental acuity as implied by the metaphor, "helmet of salvation." (Eph 6). Also pertinent to that instruction is, "Take every thought captive to the obedience of Christ." (2 Cor 10:5).

4. Memorize 1 Corinthians 13:4–7. When in doubt about what to do with another person, analyze your options and inclinations against what the Lord counts as love. We are here to learn to love as God loves; the fullness of righteousness and being like God is found in our obedience to love as he defines it.

5. Learn to talk aloud with God about what is in your heart. Speak of all that is there, both the good and the bad. This can be done during dedicated prayer time or while facing a challenging day. Adopt the tone of a dependent child when speaking to the One called "Father." Adam and God walked daily together in the Garden of Eden and conversed with one another. This story implies intimacy and trust between Adam and God. The spirit-life is the restoration of our ability to have this intimacy with God. Speak aloud, then be quiet and listen to your heart.

6. Remember, God is perfect, just, loving, and patient. If he does not appear to be answering your prayer, there are at least four possibilities of what is going on:

- You ask for something he has already provided, either in his written Word, the Bible, or by his Presence within you. He often answers prayer by simply bringing a relevant Scripture reference to the active mind. Also, recall from the discussion in "Q is for Quantum Entanglements," there is no need to ask for God to give patience, peace, or faithfulness. When feeling anxiety or anger as a result of another person, don't ask for what you lack. He has already given you the Holy Spirit, who is the fullness of all the fruits of his Spirit. Instead, ask how to draw your need from the well of his Presence. Listen for any practical thoughts that arise in the days following that prayer.

- Ask for what is needed in spirit, and recognize that what is desired by the natural self is often not aligned with actual needs at all. Learning the difference is not a problem, but it is part of the growth process. He blesses us materially and through real-life situations; however, I suggest his primary interest is in our development as emotionally stable individuals who draw guidance and strength from his Presence within.

- Some prayers are nonsensical. Some prayers hide from personal responsibility by expressing sentimental feelings in gooey-sounding words. An example is the prayer, "Change my heart, O Lord." These words acknowledge an awareness of one's failings, but ask of God to fix the heart. Has he not already given the life of his Son that we might be born of his Spirit and have a new heart? Why would a new heart born of the Divine Nature need a fix? The prayer shifts responsibility for choosing obedience off the shoulders of the supplicant and waits on God to do more. Replace "Change my heart" with an exercise of responsible initiative and ask, "Teach me in this moment. Teach me your ways for the new heart" (Ps 25: 4–5). It is a powerful step toward maturity in the spirit. Do I negate the need for God's grace and place a work-to-earn mandate between a believer and the Lord? Never. There are a multitude of imperatives on the believer detailed in the New Testament. Fulfilling any of them is a function of God's grace to give us the Holy Spirit as comforter and guide. We live standing on the grace that enables our free will to choose righteousness.
- His answer will come in his time and according to his ways. Impatience thinks he has not answered. The problem is we have not waited on him.

7. Recognize that spiritual development and growth occur across one's lifetime. There will be trials and many errors, including acting and reacting from selfishness before making the choice to follow God's way. When you fail to be true to God's Holy Spirit, confess and apologize as needed to those impacted. Move on. Recognize that the most powerful, practical action under-girding all spiritual growth is forgiveness—*of others and of oneself* (Matt 18:22; Luke 10:27).

Yielding to God honors him. The mental-emotional-physical equilibrium achieved by living in the Holy Spirit results in humility before God, effects better interaction with others, and supplies spirit-informed self-care. The Lord's Prayer is a prime example of finding the connection between our needs and the wealth of supply inherent in an authentic spirit-life. All four psychological needs examined in *Regeneration in Jesus 101*, attachment, structure/order, self-enhancement, and pleasure/pain avoidance, are addressed in the maxims of the primary prayer given by Jesus (Matt 6:9–13):

- "Our Father . . . " declares in two words our attachment to the family of believers and to God as a Father.

- "Hallowed be Your Name. Your kingdom come. Your will be done." These words speak of his Holiness as the structure of kingdom governance. Practically then, obedience to him orders one's life into the greatest possible stability. Compare this thought to Matthew 7:24–25 in the "Sermon on the Mount." The ordered structure of spirit life in union with the Holy Spirit is the life built on the rock. The house built on the rock will stand against every storm.

- "Give us this day our daily bread," is an assurance of provision for the basic needs of the physical body. This single mention of the physical body in contrast with the four spiritual aspects of the prayer implies a hierarchy of the spiritual needs above physical needs and experiences.

- "And forgive us our debts, as we also have forgiven our debtors," links with the need for self-enhancement. Granting and seeking forgiveness addresses all consequences resulting from selfish self-enhancement motives and actions.

- "And lead us not into temptation, but deliver us from evil." Pleasure, sought or known, and pain avoided are not inherently sinful. Yet, these two aspects of psychological need are frequently the source of temptations to sin. Thus "deliver us" as a supplication delves into the practicality of deciding against wrong choices. Equally important, we can be assured that the Father does not tempt us. Further, he will provide our needs in the face of the evils he hates (1 Cor 10:13; Gal 5:19–21).

Our one responsibility as a new-spirit being is "abiding in" Jesus Christ. Our life is hidden in him (Col 3:1–3). We yield by choice and discipline ourselves in the practice of abiding in him. We focus our thoughts on all things good. We manage our emotions to maintain a continual state of rest. The total practice of abiding develops our sense of union with God. Standing fully on the solid rock intellectually and emotionally, our authentic self emerges amid supernatural blessings.

Z is for Zummary
Zeal, Zone, Z-End

WE ARRIVE AT Z; our alphabetical journey nears its conclusion. One final consideration of the world in which you were born and in which our physical existence unfolds: there are fanatics. As I write this, the nation grapples with varied factions whose self-important points of view justify manipulation and deception of the general population. Fanatics are those within a group, whether followers or leaders, whose thinking becomes wholly focused on an ideological agenda, absent any care and concern for people.

Fanatics will be characterized by zeal. Zeal has both positive and negative applications. We return to the issue of what is right or wrong. Zeal for something is a passionate expression of belief for or against. Zeal manifests in determined action.

Distinguishing good zeal from bad zeal is often only a difference in perspective. Consider those 1773 Bostonians, subjects of the British Crown, who stole several chests of tea from the East India Company, a business owned by other British Crown subjects. That valuable commodity of tea, dispatched into Boston Harbor, splashed into intended ruin. In England and among colonial loyalists, the attackers inflicting the financial loss were labeled rebels and criminals. Of course, those rebels were considered patriots and heroes by the resistance-minded colonists. That group of zealous Bostonians was measured in opposite ideological terms of rebel and patriot based on one attribute, their willingness to be lawbreakers.

From the point of view of the King of England and all loyal subjects, the business of the East India Company operated as a lawful British economic endeavor. The related taxes and the sanctioned monopoly represented fair governance. Equally determined in response, the British government zealously pursued enforcement of the rule of law, a deeply held ideal. A war erupted, fueled by the opposed zealots.

What is the good or bad in the narrative of the American Revolution? Both sides claimed to be in the right. On a cultural level, many topics become divisive and lead to conflict due to new ideas developing within a population. The embrace of a new line of thought undermines the status quo of in-place governance.

Opposing views of what is good and right or what is wrong and therefore demands change are often fostered by the progress of time. A fervent advocate for any cause may be labeled a terrorist, a fanatic, a leader, or a visionary depending on one's perspective. Zealotry is frequently a force wearing subjective labels.

Words may deceive or enlighten, disparage or encourage, destroy or build individuals across the breadth of a society. The intent behind the use of words matters as much as the meaning of a word, *zeal* included.

Christian sermons are sometimes delivered with zeal, and frequently, speakers call for a congregation to exhibit zeal for God. Hitler stirred much zealous devotion from most Germans in the 1930s. In 1 John 4:1, we find an admonition to "test the spirits." John isn't talking about ghosts showing up in a believer's day to day life. People will speak from the abundance of the heart (Luke 6:45).[1] The heart, the inner being, of the human is the storehouse of spirit. It is the intent from the heart of a speaker in choosing words that matters, and the inner state being heard is what drives John to instruct on testing someone's words.

As a citizen of heaven living physically in this world, the goal of the believer is overcoming one's natural selfishness and become the new identity born of the life from God. Authentically being in God's Spirit, the abiding in the Holy Spirit, guides all other imperatives found in the Scripture for a Christian life: being a strong witness, pastor, evangelist, a good husband, a good wife, an exhorter, a prophet, or a giver. All Christian experience and choice is shaped authentically when the heart of the individual is holding to the peace of Jesus's Spirit.

We accept Jesus as God and realize the fullness of God as Father, Son, and Holy Spirit. We find an ever-deepening understanding of his goodness; yes, even that he is the *sole* source of goodness. Christians know the embrace of his Spirit in two directions: God's embrace of the believer as a new

---

1. Paraphrases adapted from the New American Standard Bible: ©2020 by the Lockman Foundation.

creature in the kingdom—he *never lets go*; and as the human embracing God—*do not ever let go* (Rom 8:35–39).

Knowing him is the equipping needed for overcoming evil. Fussing and fuming over what is wrong in ourselves and others is pointless. The antidote to all that is wrong is an active increase in the understanding and application of rightness: the goodness from God. Trying to beat bad is the proverbial beating of a dead horse. That horse will never give a ride again, eh? Selfishness cannot be made unselfish. Selfishness is broken and breaks all it touches. Attempting to overcome evil puts the focus on evil. We overcome evil with good (Rom 12:21). Seek being in the Spirit of Jesus, and doing good flows.

To this end, reading and understanding the Bible is a core action supporting the goal of walking in the new-spirit life. Practically speaking, achieving an understanding of spirit-life depends on understanding the instructions in the Bible on spirits. The written Word clearly develops a context of meaning which begins at the point of being born again in spirit. The new creature is able to receive the understanding needed to grow in spirit (2 Cor 5:17). Anyone outside the new-creature paradigm can neither intellectually nor emotionally grasp and process spirit-knowledge effectively (1 Cor 2:5–16).

The discipline of studying multiple uses of dynamic words in Scripture is a solid step toward grasping the depth of a word's meaning through the facets that are revealed. Two tools that support a deeper understanding of the Bible: an exhaustive concordance enables quick identification of all the Scriptures in which a given word appears; and before study ask God for understanding through the guidance of the Holy Spirit. Use of a concordance supports informed spiritual thinking. It is the employment of a data organizer covering the material evidence available on the nature of God, of goodness. A simple function with the complete data set is counting the usage occurrences for any given word in the Bible. This is a straightforward quantitative inquiry using the scientific protocol of observing and recording measurable data.

A practical example: using the *New American Standard Bible* and its companion concordance, check the usage frequency in the New Testament of *zeal* and *spirit*. Result: zeal is found six times (if both *zealous* and *zealot* are added, there are seventeen occurrences).[2] Spirit is found three hundred eighty-three times.[3] By those numbers, qualitative reasoning of this numerical difference regards some degree of importance for spirit over zeal.

---

2. Zondervan, *zeal*, 1339.
3. Zondervan, *spirit*, 1054–1056.

With the locations of each word's usages identified, a study of the words within context can be accomplished. The word study exercise will frequently reveal nuances of meaning, which are opportunities seized by the thoughtful reader to broaden analysis and expand inferences. It might even be said that a Christian eager to embrace this level of study is zealous for understanding the Bible and its revelations about God.

In-depth study of the Bible is work, enough work to last a lifetime. If the Bible is the textbook for living, and life is the classroom, the onus is on the believer to listen to the Teacher and apply the instructions. The premise of *Regeneration in Jesus 101* is that the evidence of spirit life on Earth resulting from a God-human connection is revealed in the Bible. That connection means a renewal of spirit life and necessarily involves a process of learning the knowledge that is based on the image of God. Colossians 3:10 reads, "and have put on the new self who is being renewed to a true knowledge according to the image of the One who created him." Knowledge as true to the image of God is what every human needs to know.

Material knowledge and related skills are taught based on three capacities of humans, technically called the cognitive, affective, and psychomotor learning domains.[4] Similarly, spirit knowledge and related practices connect the mind, heart, and body. (The Bible also develops content describing the soul, which is not included in the domains of learning.) Learning in material human terms may serve as a model for acquiring spiritual knowledge. Human understanding of the learning process includes the work of Benjamin Bloom. Paraphrasing from Bloom's Taxonomy of Learning, find a distinct pattern of development in all learning:

- Assimilate basic content knowledge from a text, instructor expertise, or both.
- Gain comprehension of content through experiential activities.
- Practice skill-set applications in relevant, varied formats.
- Engage in analysis/responsive use of the skills in a controlled setting.
- Use proficient, creative skill application in open-ended, real-life situations.
- Learning extends through continuing evaluation of outcome efficacy.[5]

---

4. Ruhl, Charlotte, "Bloom's Taxonomy of Learning."
5. Ruhl, Charlotte, "Bloom's Taxonomy of Learning."

Z is for Zummary

The same ordering of levels may be applied to living the Christian spirit-life:

- A spirit-life learner reads the Bible and receives instruction from more mature believers to build basic content knowledge.
- The spirit learner accepts daily life as the classroom of hands-on experience and determines to build comprehension of self as a regenerated person.
- Practicing the development of skill sets, such as raising questions, self-reflection, focused prayer, and stilled meditation, fosters relevant analysis of personal spirit growth as an ongoing life experience.
- Applications of being in the spirit include truth-illuminated thinking and emotionally regenerated tonal inflection, and these manifest in response to the trials of everyday pressures and interactions with other people.
- Spiritual maturity is the creative and proficient expression of love, joy, peace, patience, kindness, goodness, faithfulness, gentleness, and self-control in all circumstances.
- Self-evaluation of outcomes opens the child of God to the Refiner's fire and the Potter's affirmations, which are the backbone of "ripening fruit" also known as sanctification.

(A caveat is that trial and error is part of the learning process. Errors are expected at any level but most common in the earlier stages.)

Any individual intentionally focused on using a skill creates a mental space governing what is being accomplished. That focused mental space, particularly when all-encompassing and productive of notable outcomes, has gained a commonly used descriptor, "in the zone." For the Christian, such mental-space focus is to set the mind on the things above, not on the things of this world (Col 3:2). A Christian "in the zone" is the one who practices being in the spirit. The believer maintains a mental space that supports productivity and the notable outcomes of spiritual fruit.

There is only one imperative in Romans 12 suggesting zeal for God, "Be fervent in spirit." Here, being zealous for God and in the spirit overlap and become synonymous with another scriptural imperative directly from Jesus, abide. John 15:4 reads, "Abide in Me, and I in you. As the branch cannot bear fruit of itself unless it abides in the vine, so neither can you unless you abide in Me."

God is spirit. Being in the spirit, we begin the journey of becoming the **Authentic** self God intended for all in the beginning. **Belief** in Jesus is the Foundation of our spiritual life, and sensitivity to one's **Conscience** builds our connection to the Holy Spirit within us. **Death** of the body becomes nothing to fear, since we know our worth in God's eyes and our destiny in him.

As spirit-born humans, we are already alive for **Eternity**. We experience **Freedom** as the exercise of will empowered by a developing spiritual maturity. We practice **Gratitude** every day in every circumstance as a primary lesson in recognizing being in the spirit. Like gratitude, all aspects of the Christian experience, from spirit-birth through spirit-maturation, turn on one's **Humility** before the Lord God. In humility, we accept Jesus's instruction to become like a little child. The warmth and wonder of spiritual **Intimacy** with God stands on the phrase "a child of God."

Knowing that Jesus **Judges** all strengthens us spiritually to resist unrighteous judgmentalism and protects us from being harmed by it. Self-sacrificing love underpins the Christian relational experience and enables the deepest sense of belonging in the group: **Kingdom** kinship. The spirit-filled love between fellow believers is another gift from God.

The **Life** of Jesus indwells a human through the Holy Spirit and supports the maturation of the believer's new spirit. Born of the spirit and living therein is the **Meaning** of Christianity. Maturing as a person is a direct result of overcoming **Negative** behavioral habits that root in the old nature, often from unmet psychological needs.

We choose **Obedience** to God. Willful obedience is the spiritual effect that results from loving God. **Perseverance** in small, accessible moments of challenge teaches us discipline and strength, the living in the spirit. Thereby, we prepare for tribulation or persecution in the future. These two are predicted for us as the Apocalypse unfolds.

To seek, knock, and ask is the ultimate **Quest** by the spirit-being to know, understand, and live in the life of God. That quest includes learning responsive action to God, the entering the **Rest** in God. Finding that place of rest is an emotional state enabling intentional dying to selfishness. This is a fundamental **Self-discipline**. Self-discipline over sensual desire is a service of worship for God.

The absolute **Truth** in the Bible renews the mind and empowers love through the work of the Holy Spirit in us. That truth engages us through our **Union** with God. From this union, we determine to manifest **Virtue**, the good we have and give freely. In his Spirit, our spirit speaks and acts with grace, compassion, mercy, truth, hope, faith and love.

Living in spirit, we gain **W**isdom, the sound judgment from God that guides the will and governs all desire. That wisdom is built on Jesus, the All in All. He is the gift of the power of eternal life and the source of righteous life on Earth. We e**X**alt him above all else. **Y**ielding daily and abiding in Jesus through the indwelling Presence is the practice of real-time Christianity, the journey into a mature being reflecting Jesus. Be **Z**ealous to live, move, and have your being in him. Be fervent in spirit.

ZEE-END

Here in North Carolina, the state motto is "Esse Quam Videri." Translated from Latin, it is "To be, rather than to seem." It is your choice to accept the Bible as the truth, absolute and complete. It is a distinct move of your own will to accept Jesus and commit to belonging to God. If that is your choice, then be a Christian by living aware of your spiritual inner being in communion with the Holy Spirit. There are no viable substitutes—no hacks whatsoever. Seeming to be a Christian by keeping a personal construct of good behavior standards will never satisfy God's longing for you or meet the needs of your heart. Be the human born of the Spirit of God, who chooses abiding in the fullness of Jesus's Spirit, the divine design for the human heart, soul, mind, and body.

Bibliography

Armstead, Theresa L., et al. "Structural and Social Determinants of Inequities in Violence Risk: A Review of Indicators." PubMed Central, accessed May 19, 2025. https://pmc.ncbi.nlm.nih.gov/articles/PMC7278040/.

ESA. "Giant Iceberg Breaks Away From Antarctic Ice Shelf." European Space Agency, accessed January 15, 2024. https://www.esa.int/Applications/Observing_the_Earth/Copernicus/Giant_iceberg_breaks_away_from_Antarctic_ice_shelf.

Flaherty, Colleen. 2021. "Controversial Scholar Resigns." *Inside Higher Ed*. https://www.insidehighered.com/news/2021/11/28/controversial-scholar-pedophilia-resigns-old-dominion.

Grawe, Klaus. *Neuropsychotherapy: How the Neuroscience Informs Effective Psychotherapy*. New York: Taylor & Francis Group, 2007.

Grudin, Robert. "Humanism | Definition, Principles, History, & Influence." *Britannica*, accessed September 29, 2024. https://www.britannica.com/topic/humanism .

Hendricks, Scotty. "10 Schools of Philosophy and Why You Should Know Them." Big Think. https://bigthink.com/thinking/10-schools-of-philosophy-and-why-you-should-know-them/.

Henriques, Gregg, PhD. "What is the Relationship Between Psychology and Psyche?" *Psychology Today*, accessed February 25, 2024. https://www.psychologytoday.com/us/blog/theory-of-knowledge/202402/what-is-the-relationship-between-psychology-and-the-psyche?msockid=1cbb8f0a237c662730f39ad7229667c9

IHEU. "'IHEU Minimum Statement on Humanism,' Humanists International, General Assembly, 1996." Humanists International, accessed October 25, 2023. https://humanists.international/policy/iheu-minimum-statement-on-humanism/.

Jefferson, Thomas. "The Declaration of Independence." National Archives. April 25, 2024. https://www.archives.gov/founding-docs/declaration.

Key, A. P. "What is neurotic behavior?" WebMD, accessed May 14, 2025. https://www.webmd.com/mental-health/neurotic-behavior-overview.

McEvoy, Shawn, ed. "Apokalupsis Meaning—Greek Lexicon | New Testament (NAS)." Bible Study Tools, accessed January 21, 2025. https://www.biblestudytools.com/lexicons/greek/nas/apokalupsis.html.

Bibliography

———. "Christos Meaning—Greek Lexicon | New Testament (NAS)." Bible Study Tools, accessed February 06, 2025. https://www.biblestudytools.com/lexicons/greek/nas/christos.html.

McGrath, Alister E. *Christian Theology: An Introduction*. 3rd ed. Oxford: Blackwell, 2001.

Merriam-Webster's Collegiate Dictionary. 10th ed. Springfield, MA: Merriam-Webster, 1994.

"Projection." *Psychology Today*, accessed December 19, 2024. https://www.psychologytoday.com/us/basics/projection.

Ruhl, Charlotte. "Bloom's Taxonomy of Learning." Simply Psychology. https://www.simplypsychology.org/blooms-taxonomy.html.

Smithsonian Institution. "The Beatles' First Appearance on 'The Ed Sullivan Show,'" accessed March 1, 2023. https://www.si.edu/newsdesk/snapshot/beatles-first-appearance-ed-sullivan-show.

Zondervan NASB Exhaustive Concordance. Grand Rapids: Zondervan, 2000.

www.ingramcontent.com/pod-product-compliance
Lightning Source LLC
Chambersburg PA
CBHW071213160426
43196CB00011B/2280